# Heirpower!
## Eight Basic Habits of Exceptionally Powerful Lieutenants

BOB VÁSQUEZ
Chief Master Sergeant, USAF, Retired

Air University Press
Maxwell Air Force Base, Alabama

June 2006

**Air University Library Cataloging Data**

Vásquez, Bob.

Heirpower! : eight basic habits of exceptionally powerful lieutenants / Bob Vásquez.

p. ; cm.

1. Command of troops. 2. Leadership. I. Title.

355.33041—dc22

**Disclaimer**

Air University Press
131 West Shumacher Avenue
Maxwell AFB AL 36112-6615
http://aupress.maxwell.af.mil

# Contents

# Foreword

Chief Bob Vásquez has found an innovative and effective way to share some basic principles that every new lieutenant should know on the subject of how to succeed as a leader in our great Air Force. He provides the enlisted perspective in a way that only a senior noncommissioned officer can communicate. I've known the chief for many years and have seen him succeed as an enlisted leader and as a mentor to the many officers he's served. As a member of the Air Force Academy's Center for Character Development, he mentors our future leaders on a daily basis. It is obvious that serving is his passion. I'm convinced that any lieutenant who reads this book will be better prepared to lead at every level.

RONALD R. FOGLEMAN, General, USAF, Retired
Durango, Colorado
9 March 2006

The odds are that most of us who have served lengthy careers as senior noncommissioned officers in the Air Force have sage advice to share with fledgling officers. The difference is that Chief Bob Vásquez has done it—in a well-written, common-sense how-to book. Easy to read and appropriately interspersed with humorous guidance, *Heirpower!* is not just for new lieutenants, but for anyone in a position of leadership. I've known Bob for over 30 years. Not only does he talk this stuff, he practices it daily—and it works. After you read *Heirpower!* do what he says, and you'll be an *exceptional* leader.

ROBERT D. GAYLOR, Chief Master Sergeant of the Air Force, Retired
San Antonio, Texas
18 January 2006

# *About the Author*

Bob Vásquez is currently the course director for the freshman seminar Vital Effective Character through Observation and Reflection (VECTOR), offered through the US Air Force Academy's Center for Character Development. He served in the Air Force for more than 30 years before retiring on 1 November 2002. Bob invested 24 of those years in Air Force bands throughout the world. He also served as commandant of the Noncommissioned Officer Academy at March AFB, California; senior enlisted advisor to the commander of the 92nd Airlift Wing at Fairchild AFB, Washington; deputy director of the Family Support Center at Ramstein AB, Germany; and superintendent for the 86th Mission Support Group at Ramstein. A proud member of the Air Force Academy's team since 16 November 2002, Bob is also an adjunct professor at the University of Colorado at Colorado Springs. Although he is an author as well as a musician, speaker, life coach, and mentor, Bob considers his greatest accomplishments the raising of his daughters, Tesa and Elyse, a granddaughter, Nieves, and growing closer to Debbie, his lovely bride of more than 28 wonderful and fulfilling years.

# *Preface*

Isn't this a great day to be an American warrior? If I had a dime for every time I've said that, I'd be driving a BMW. Wait a minute! I drive *two* BMWs! I've gained some notoriety from that statement, but that's not why I say it—nor why I developed it. It's a sincere statement of loyalty and dedication to a way of life I enjoyed for most of my adult days. I've written this book to share my experiences and joy with you and to help you be your best because I believe that if you're an effective officer/leader (aka an Exceptionally Powerful Lieutenant), you will certainly take care of a group of people I love dearly: enlisted folks. I'm not sure you got the enlisted perspective from the institution where you received your commission, but you're going to get it now! In a good way, of course. My goal is to empower you with habits that will make you an Exceptionally Powerful Lieutenant. What I'll share with you comes from an enlisted perspective. Don't throw away what you already know about leading; just add this material to your toolbox.

But enough about you; let's talk about me. I served in the United States Air Force for more than 30 great years. The official line is that I retired in 2002, but the term *retirement* carries a tinge of volunteerism. I did not volunteer to leave my service. I would have stayed another 30 years had I been afforded that opportunity. I love serving with people whose purpose lies beyond their own desires and who do everything in their power to keep our country free.

I served in the rank of chief master sergeant (E-9) for almost 12 years—more than a third of my service time—and, as such, had many opportunities to mentor officers of every grade and every rank of enlisted person. I can't tell you how many lieutenants I chewed up and spit out! (Okay, I never did that, but it sounded good and got your attention, right?) Speaking of which, I still always stand at attention for lieutenants, who have a special place in my heart because they're the first officers who lead my enlisted brethren. I'm convinced that that first leadership opportunity sets the stage for the rest of an officer's military life, eventually leading him or her to become either a good or bad senior officer. I hope that this book will help you become a good senior officer.

What gives me the right to make the assertions I do in this book? As I assessed my answer to that question, I tried to remember when I started leading people. It was almost easier to remember when I *didn't* lead. I've led for as long as my memory will take me back. That in itself doesn't make me an authority, I know. I've also observed and studied countless leaders, taking note of what worked and what didn't work for them. I was blessed with working with both the best and the worst. I learned a great deal from both types.

You may not agree with what you read here, and you're welcome to argue with me if you please. I can assure you that what you're about to read is the truth as I know it. My hope is that you'll laugh, cry, and learn as I share some basic leadership ideas with you that will make you an Exceptionally Powerful Lieutenant. Now, go forward! Make this a great day to be an American warrior. ¡Adelante!

BOB VÁSQUEZ, Chief Master Sergeant, USAF, Retired
Monument, Colorado
1 January 2006

# Acknowledgments

Everything we do in this world is touched by someone else. I'm grateful to everyone who has nurtured me and given me opportunities to excel and to fail. I learned from every experience. The following is only a partial list of those to whom I owe much. There are many more, but it would take another book just to mention them.

Thanks to Dr. Russ Sojourner; Maj Jeff Kozyra; Col Tom Berry, USAF, retired; Maj Gen Gary Dylewski, USAF, retired; and my colleagues at the US Air Force Academy's Center for Character Development who continuously support me in making my vision a reality.

Thanks to my personal life coaches who continuously show me the way: Mr. D. J. "Eagle Bear" Vanas, Mr. Noah benShea, and Ms. Sarah Hurd.

Thanks to the officers who have mentored and inspired me through the years: Gen Ron Fogleman, USAF, retired; Maj Gen Gary Voellger, USAF, retired, and his lovely bride, Carroll; Lt Gen Stephen Lorenz; Lt Gen Art Lichte; Col Denny Layedecker; Maj Doug Monroe; Maj Hank Emerson, USAF, retired; Capt Eric Carrano; and all of the lieutenants, too many to list, with whom I stood to make a positive difference.

Thanks to the chiefs who made me a chief: CMSgt John Sterle, USAF, retired; Chief Master Sergeant of the Air Force (CMSAF) Bob Gaylor, retired; CMSAF Dave Campanale, retired; CMSAF Paul Airey, retired; CMSAF Bud Andrews, deceased; CMSAF Sam Parish, retired; CMSAF Jim McCoy, retired; CMSAF Jim Binnicker, retired; CMSgt Bob Smith, USAF, retired; CMSgt Roy Boudreau, USAF, retired; CMSgt Ron White, USAF, retired; CMSgt Frank Guidas, USAF, retired; CMSgt Mac McVicar, USAF, deceased; CMSgt George Moriarty, USAF, retired; and CMSgt Jose Tavarez, USAF, retired.

Thanks to all the cadets who have passed through the US Air Force Academy. Those I've known are the real inspiration behind this book. They are the best and brightest who endure much more than I ever could so that they can fulfill their dreams of being warriors and defenders of our way of life and freedom.

Thanks to Mom, Dad, Tio Rulie, Momma Joyce, and my siblings—particularly my baby sister, Elva—for providing me the love and nurturing I needed to succeed as a warrior.

Thanks to the two teachers who empowered me to grow—Mr. Bruce Firkins and Mr. Jack Hall—and to my editor at Air University Press, Dr. Marvin Bassett, who helped make sense of what I've written.

Special thanks to Debbie, my lovely bride of 28 wonderful and fulfilling years, who keeps me on the right track; who has endured all of the assignments, TDYs, and late-night calls; and who gave me the greatest gift of all: my daughters, Tesa and Elyse. Thanks to Nieves, my grandbaby, who gives me different eyes with which to see this wonderful world.

Lastly and mostly, I thank my God at least twice a day for the blessings I receive every day. I'll never be worthy, but I accept them as grace.

# Introduction

You may be wondering how I chose the title of this book: *Heirpower! Eight Basic Habits of Exceptionally Powerful Lieutenants.* Or you may not. Here's the explanation anyway. I'll break it down one word at a time because I believe words are very powerful. It may help if you understand the words in the title because they bind the text into my purpose for sharing these thoughts with you—to help you become an Exceptionally Powerful Lieutenant. A *lieutenant* is a *leader*—or is expected to be one—so please forgive me if I use those terms interchangeably. By the way, although the title may sound similar to others you may have read, the content is not. Believe me!

The concept of *heirpower* is simple. An *heir* is a *successor.* If you break that word apart, you're left with *success* and *or.* Success or. . . . The alternative to success is failure. What you'll find in this book deals with success—not failure. Better yet, it's about enabling people to succeed. *Power* is the capacity to act effectively. Who has power? You do! I do! We all do! Real power is produced when we share what we have. In this book, I share all that I can with you that will enable you to succeed. We'll achieve real success when you take what I give you and what you develop on your own and then share it with others. The only way to get is to give. The best way to succeed is to help others succeed. Pass on all you can, and you too will develop heirpower.

Why the number *eight*? My daughters used to watch a television program called *Schoolhouse Rock.* They loved that show. Okay, *I* loved that show, so they had to watch it. One of the show's songs—about the figure eight—caught my attention. One of the lyrics went, "Figure eight as double four . . . that's a circle that turns 'round upon itself." What's that got to do with leadership? Well, CMSgt Gene Gardner, USAF, retired, an old friend of mine, once told me that "as leaders, we can do one of two things: we can do something *to* our people or we can do something *for* our people." Now, as we get to know each other through this book, you'll find that I enjoy playing with words, so let me take his statement and make it more powerful. Isn't *for* (four) twice as much as *to* (two)? Hence, eight will be even twice as powerful as four (for), right? If that doesn't make sense, don't worry about it. I'll probably tell you more things that don't make sense on the surface. You'll just have to trust that I know what I'm trying to tell you. You'll also find that I like circles. The figure eight—a circle that turns 'round upon itself—is powerful too. You'll find at the end of this book that these concepts all turn 'round upon themselves. They're simple but important, and they all almost blend into each other. Leadership is a cycle that continues indefinitely. More on that later. I think that by employing eight important leadership lessons, you will become an exceptional leader.

The term *basic* is, well, basic. I studied with a professor who told me that life is simple, once you understand its complexities. I told you that my purpose is to help you become an Exceptionally Powerful Lieutenant. An important question is, Who will you lead? Yourself and other people! Pretty simple, don't you think? Maybe not. People are complex entities. You're a complex being, aren't you? We even take pride in that sometimes. Leadership, I believe, is much simpler than we often think. The problem, really, is that we *don't* think—neither very much nor very often. When we do, it's not always about what we should be thinking about. As you read this book's eight admonishments, you may say, "Hey, I knew that!" That's okay. I don't profess to be a prophet. I'm just trying to guide you to think about what will help you become an Exceptionally Powerful Lieutenant. You already know this stuff. You just haven't thought of it lately. See how basic that is? Or is it too complex?

I believe Aristotle said, "We are what we repeatedly do." Dr. Stephen Covey, author of *The Seven Habits of Highly Effective People* (Yeah, it sounds like the title of this book, but don't forget I told you the content is different—so read on), says that we first build our habits, and then our habits build us. There's much truth to what both these sages say. The more we do something, the better we become at doing it. That TV ad that says "Just do it!" doesn't necessarily have any thought behind it. I'm hoping that this book will first make you think about *why* you *should* do it *before* you do it. And then you can *do it right* and you can *do it now!* I'll even tell you what *it* is. *Habits,* like words, are very powerful in that eventually you won't even think about what you're doing. You'll make things happen almost naturally—habitually.

In the paragraph that follows, I explain what *powerful* means, but before I get to that, let me ask you, Are you the type of person who just wants to make the grade? Are you comfortable simply meeting the standard? Or are you willing to do what it takes to achieve your personal best in all you do? Do you see yourself setting the standard for excellence? If you answered yes to the first two questions, then go read a Marvel comic book. If you answered yes to the second two, then read on. You're going to be a great leader! An *exceptional* leader! You see, to lead the enlisted folks we recruit these days, you're going to have to be way above ordinary. Just meeting the standard will not be good enough. Your troops won't follow you unless they believe you're better than they are. The eight habits I'm about to share with you will set you above everyone else. By living them, you will be—I guarantee—not only powerful, but *exceptionally* powerful.

We use the term *powerful* fairly regularly. Do you know what it means? I'm going to bet that you've never even thought about what it means. Let me help you out. *Powerful* means *full of power*. Basically, that's what it means, doesn't it? One dictionary defines *full* as "containing all that is normal or possible." *Power*, it says, is "the ability or capacity to perform or act effectively." According to Covey, "*effectiveness* is getting what you want again and again and again." You are full of power! You have within you all of the capacity you need to inspire your troops to follow you. We'll dismiss the word *normal* in the definition of *full* because you're not willing to settle for normal. You'll set a higher standard for those you lead because you have the desire and the will to do it. This book's eight lessons are basic to powerful leadership. If you do them and make them habits, you will get what you want—the respect and loyalty of your enlisted troops—over and over again. Know this: power is not control. The only person you *may* control is you, and good luck with that! Real power lies in knowing what the people you lead need and want—and providing it to them so that you can all grow together. The lessons from this book will empower you to do that.

If you develop these eight habits, I assure you that you will succeed as a leader, particularly a leader of enlisted people. The enlisted men and women you lead will follow you and nurture you. If you haven't heard this next statement already, you will soon: "The enlisted corps is the backbone of our military forces." Enlisted folks have a different function than officers, but they have the same value. Leaders must realize that they cannot do everything and, in truth, can do nothing without the support of their enlisted people. Lieutenants lead enlisted people—not officers. An effective lieutenant does the eight things I'm about to share with you. Read this book. Learn what it says. Do it on a daily basis. And enjoy the ride!

Oh, you're thinking I left out an explanation of the last word of the title—*lieutenants*. Believe it or not, that was intentional. Up until the day you walk into your first—or new—assignment, everyone will have a vision of what a lieutenant is. That vision is not necessarily positive. My hope is that, having read this book and having made a commitment to follow its tenets, you will redefine what people think a lieutenant is—and can be. You will be so good that when you leave your unit, people will say, "That was one Exceptionally Powerful Lieutenant!"

## Words of Wisdom

*The secret of your future is hidden in your daily routine.*

—Mike Murdock

*A lie has speed, but truth has endurance.*

—Edgar J. Mohn

*What we have done for ourselves alone dies with us; what we have done for others and the world remains and is immortal.*

—Albert Pike

*Don't be the best in the world. Be the best for the world.*

—Dewitt Jones

*Power is the ability to do good things for others.*

—Brooke Astor

*The most powerful weapon on earth is the human soul on fire.*

—Field Marshal Ferdinand Foch

*Rank does not confer privilege or give power. It imposes responsibility.*

—Peter Drucker

*Today is the tomorrow you looked forward to yesterday.*

—Unknown

So you're 22 years old, you've just gotten your commission, you've arrived at your first duty station, you've met with your commander, and you're now "in charge" of a group of enlisted men and women, all of whom have been in service longer than you, know a whole lot more about military life than you, and are expecting more than you know. To top it all off, your first "subordinate" happens to be a 30-year veteran of every war you ever read about, and his rank is, yes, E-9. He's not an E-10 only because that rank doesn't exist. Now what do you do? Let me tell you. . . .

Habit 1

# Get a Haircut!
### First Impressions Last

"Great news, Warriors!" the commander says excitedly, "I brought you all here today to introduce you to your new leader. You all know we've been looking forward to this for a long time. Please do all you can to make the lieutenant comfortable."

This is the day you've been waiting for. After months—even years—of preparation, you've finally made it. You are the leader. The commander has pumped you up. You've pumped yourself up. You're anticipating that your followers will be as excited to see you as the commander obviously is. You are ready!

Oh, wait. As you climb the steps to the podium, you get a glimpse of the crowd gathered to greet you, and you see something different than you expected. They're not happy. What can they be thinking? "Aw, man!" the enlisted folks are thinking (actually, they're saying it), "Another green lieutenant. Here we go again!"

When you reach the podium, you look out at the troops and see a change of face. You might as well be wearing a superhero outfit because you are tight (for you older lieutenants, that means sharp). You look good. Your hair is perfectly coifed (combed, for you less worldly folks) and tapered beyond standards. Your uniform is so crisp that it snaps, crackles, and pops (yes, I'm making reference to Rice Krispies). Your shoes are so shiny they compete with the glare from the Old Man's bald head. I mean, as you walk onto the stage, the theme music from *Rocky* starts blaring out of the intercom speakers. Okay, wake up!

I was about to say that I hope your first duty day is like what I just described. The truth is that you can *make* it that way. It takes work though. As I tried to emphasize in describing the word *habits* in this book's title, the idea is to do what's right so often that it becomes habitual. You don't even have to think about it—you just do it. Interestingly, that clause is closely related to Nike products. You may not know it, but Nike was the

Greek goddess of victory. (Okay, so you did know that. Hey, I'm trying to impress you here!) Victory in life comes from developing good habits. Being good often begins with looking good, and your troops will expect you to look at least as good as they do. Now think a little bit. As the leader, don't you think you should look even better than the people you lead? Hmmm.

Whatever first impression you make on your troops, whatever they think you look like the first time they meet you, will stay in their minds forever. First impressions last. One of the reasons we insist that our military members be clean shaven, wear their uniforms properly, wear their hats outdoors, and so forth, is that it presents a professional military image. You are a professional, aren't you? You are in the military, at least for the next several years, right? Your personal appearance will set the standard for your unit. What you give, you'll get. If you look good, chances are your troops will emulate you. If you look sloppy, chances are your troops will emulate you. That's the truth. So make it a habit to *look your best, not just good, every day.* Be exceptional!

You'll also make an impression by the language you use. The military doesn't condone the use of vulgar language. Guess who has to impose that? You! Again, you can't enforce that rule if you break it yourself. Vulgar language validates a person's ignorance and disrespect for others. The American language includes myriad terms that you can use to provide the emphasis that vulgar words do. People use offensive language because it becomes habitual. Most of the time, they don't even realize they're offending anyone—but they are. Even if the offended ones don't say so. Live up to the standard of leaders, and get rid of vulgarities in your speech. Think about this: where do vulgar words come from? Vulgar minds. Get rid of vulgar thoughts, and you'll get rid of vulgar words. Don't use them! Remember, you are now a leader— a professional leader. Think like one, and speak like one.

Your troops will be looking out for if—and how—you respect them. If you want to start out on the wrong foot, call them all by their first names. If you want to impress them, call them by their ranks and last names. Remember, you're setting the standard. What may happen, depending on the professionalism of the group, is that they'll ask you to call them by their first names. You make the call. Is that a professional habit to develop? It may depend on the maturity and trust levels within the unit. Nonetheless, don't take it upon yourself to call your followers by their first names. If they give you permission to do so, consider it deeply before you do it. And *never* give a follower permission to call *you* by your first name! I've often heard people say they have different rules when they're "off duty." "It's okay to call each other by first name when we're having a drink," they say. More on that later. First, you're never off duty. Most importantly, if you try to be different at work and at play, you'll eventually mess up. I've been there way too often. Remember, you'll do what you practice.

You'll also impress your troops, at least the professional ones, by the way you salute. I'm amazed at the different types of salutes I see officers render. Okay, often enlisted folks aren't much better. I'll admonish them in another book. *Your salute sends a clear message about how much pride you take in your profession.* The military profession is the only one in which people salute each other regularly. Your salute says a lot about how you view discipline. I'll tell you more about that subject in a later chapter. A shabby salute says you don't care. That's the truth. If you salute proudly, sharply, and appropriately, your troops will see that you mean business when it comes to military bearing. Oh, one more thing on saluting: don't thank an enlisted person for saluting you. You'll never find an enlisted person thanking an officer for returning a salute. It's a sign of mutual respect. Leave it at that.

Is it possible to make a bad first impression but repair it? It is, but it will take much work and probably much time. You can repent and do all sorts of good things for your folks, and they may show you respect. But know this: if you ever do anything dumb, they will revert to their first impression of you. "I always knew the lieutenant was a dirtbag. I remember the first time I saw her. I knew she was bad!" That's what will go through their minds and their lips. Trust me! I've been there.

Here's the lesson: look good, speak well, be respectful, and salute sharply. Start now to develop these habits. Pay attention to whether or not you present a professional military image. Ask someone you trust—not necessarily a buddy—to help you. Make sure you look your best all the time—even off duty—because when your troops see you downtown, they will talk about you back at the shop. Help them say good things about you. If the people you hang with use vulgar language, either make them quit or find new friends. The only way to gain respect is to give it, so treat your troops with respect on and off duty. Be proud of your profession, and express that fact continuously. If you need to practice your salute, stand in front of a mirror and do it. But do it right! Remember that old saying "Practice makes perfect"? Wrong! Practice makes permanent. If you practice doing something badly, you'll soon be doing it badly—but perfectly bad! I think you get the picture.

You'll find two types of enlisted folks in your unit: those who need you to lead them and those who can lead *you*. I'll tell you more about the latter in the last chapter, but consider the former now. They need you to lead them in the right direction. In the past, I would have admonished you to aim high. What the heck, aim high! Make your standard continue to rise by raising it; your troops will raise it by following you. Gen George S. Patton said, "You are always on parade." Your troops, peers, and leaders are watching you. You have the capacity to excel. Don't just do it; do it right! Stand tall! First impressions last!

## War Story

My troops came to me asking for help. I call them my troops, but they actually belonged to someone else several layers of leadership away from me. They didn't have a chief to go to, so they came to me. Their noncommissioned officer in charge (NCOIC) and I had this conversation:

NCOIC: "You have to do something, Chief!"

Me: "What's the problem?"

NCOIC: "It's the new lieutenant!"

Me: "What's wrong with him?"

NCOIC: "He's having us go through open-ranks inspections! He comes around the shops with a white glove on, inspecting our tools and our areas. He expects us to wear clean uniforms every day. Since the first day he got here, he's just been a real jerk, Chief!"

Me: "It sounds to me as though he's trying to raise the standard in your organization. Can you honestly say that what he's expecting you to live up to is bad for your unit?"

NCOIC: "No, Sir."

4

Me: "Maybe the problem is that your folks have become complacent, so now this new lieutenant's vision of your potential is going against that and you're having a hard time dealing with getting back on track." (Man, I was being brilliant!)

NCOIC: "Chief, would you come over and check it out for yourself?"

Me: "Sure."

I did go by. I met the new lieutenant. He looked terrible. Oh, he was wearing a clean uniform, but he surely had slept in it the night before. I know, I know, you're not supposed to starch the BDU, but you should at least iron it before you wear it. His hair was interesting—not exactly a Jheri Curl, but someone must have made plenty of money selling pomade to this man. It was slick all right, but it obviously was holding in the hair so that it didn't look as long as it was. And his language! First of all, he befriended me immediately. Now, I don't want to give you the impression that I'm a snob or that chiefs can't be friendly, but when I introduced myself as "Bob Vásquez," he took it seriously! He called me "Bob"! Mentor that I am, I quickly straightened him out. Senior leaders often introduce themselves by name, not rank. It's a form of humility. But *never* take that as permission to use their first names!

What was this first impression? Mine was negative, to say the least, and that's the way I saw him. Is that fair? Not necessarily, but it's true!

I hate it when I'm wrong, don't you? Luckily, I was only partially wrong. I asked him about the inspections, and he explained that there was a tremendous amount of work to be done to meet safety standards and that the shop was very disorganized. He had honorable and sincere intentions. He just hadn't read this book, so he didn't know about habit 8 (you will soon). The poor guy was trying his best. He just needed some guidance.

I asked him about his language. "That's how my troops talk, Chief," he explained. You see, he may have been disheveled, but he wasn't dumb. (Notice how he quickly started calling me by my real first name—"Chief.") I gave him the sermon on how that type of language brings down the level of professionalism within a group. He understood and apologized. He was just trying to fit in. Actually, I think he was relieved to have my support for not using vulgarities.

5

After I gathered the NCOs, we talked about what I'd learned. They seemed to understand where the lieutenant was coming from. He'd just started on the wrong foot. Although he thought he'd impress them with his vision, making the unit better, the troops were unimpressed with their vision of him. He didn't look the part of a leader, so they didn't see him as such. Eventually, with some mentoring, that lieutenant became one of the wing's best. He took a different approach to leading that led to his troops respecting him and even following him. Was the troops' first impression still with them? Yes, but that lieutenant worked so hard to fix it that he never messed up as long as he was there. The troops never had to revert to their first impression.

You may have the best of intentions. You may have the best message ever thought of. You may have the solution to all of your troops' woes. But if you don't deliver it right the first time, it will never take effect. *First impressions last!*

## Starting Points

I think that the first step toward developing a good habit starts with a good question. As Paul A. Samuelson said, "Good questions outrank easy answers." According to Naguib Mahfouz, "You can tell whether a man is clever by his answers. You can tell whether a man is wise by his questions." At the end of each habit, I provide you some questions—some starting points—that you should consider if you choose to develop the habit just discussed. I don't necessarily have the answers on specifically how you can improve, only because each situation calls for a different response. I will, however, provide you a way to reach me so that I can help you (see "Final Thoughts"). I hope these questions will point you in the right direction. Some wise guy once said something to the effect that the answers are always within the questions. Okay, maybe I just made that up. I have been called a wise guy before. Think! Question! Do! Be!

- How would the person I would like to be do what I am about to do?
- Do I look like a professional leader?
- Do I speak like a professional leader?
- Do I think like an Exceptionally Powerful Lieutenant?

# Words of Wisdom

*Vision without action is a daydream. Action without vision is a nightmare.*

—Japanese proverb

*The game of life is the game of boomerangs. Our thoughts, deeds, and words return to us sooner or later, with astounding accuracy.*

—Florence Shinn

*Ordinary people believe only in the possible. Extraordinary people visualize not what is possible or probable, but rather what is impossible. And by visualizing the impossible, they begin to see it as possible.*

—Cherie Carter-Scott

*Your talk talks and your walk talks, but your walk talks louder than your talk talks.*

—John C. Maxwell

*The man who radiates good cheer, who makes life happier wherever he meets it, is always a man of vision and faith.*

—Ella Wheeler Wilcox

*Leadership is the capacity to translate vision into reality.*

—Warren Bennis

*The empires of the future are empires of the mind.*

—Winston Churchill

Habit 2

# Shut Up!
### Listen and Pay Attention

So you're now a lieutenant! A leader of men and women! People look up to you. Okay, *some* people look up to you. As the leader, you and others think, for some unknown reason, that you possess knowledge and wisdom. So they come to you for guidance. Since you are their leader and your purpose is to help your troops out as much as you can, you're more than willing to do so when a teammate comes to you with a problem.

"Lieutenant, I need your help," she says. "Aw, this is good," you think, "She respects me enough to seek my counsel." She just started talking, and you're already thinking of something else—about how to fix her "problem." Your heart is in the right place, but your brain is already wandering, searching the recesses of your mind, trying to formulate an answer. You, like most of us, are good at jumping to solutions. The problem is that you don't know what the problem is. You aren't listening. You may be hearing—and that's questionable—but you're hearing with the intent to reply. That's not listening.

In enlisted professional military education, we teach the troops a three-step communication process: tell them what you're going to tell them, tell them, and then tell them what you told them. That process works well if you're giving a briefing or teaching a class, but no one uses it to ask for help. Normally, the first part of the conversation is either background, icebreaker, or diversion. The punch line comes at the end of the conversation. If you stop listening as soon as you assume (and you know what that does) you know the question, chances are you'll provide a perfect answer to a totally different question. What's really bad is that since you know it's the perfect answer, you'll start patting yourself on the back early in the conversation and call it a success. In the meantime, your troop is still talking.

"Wait a minute!" you say. "I'll validate that my troop under-stands the answer I give her and that it does answer the ques-tion. I'll do that by asking her if she understands." Think a little bit. The troop is young and inexperienced. She's less experi-enced than you are. She came to you because she respects you. Surely, she had some trepidation—if not downright fear, mixed with awe—about coming to you in the first place. You ask her (with all sincerity, of course), "Do you understand?" What do you expect that youngster to answer? Maybe, "Nah, man, you're not even close to answering my question. Did you stop listening? Can't you do better than that?" I think not. She's going to an-swer, whether it's true or not, "Yes, Lieutenant!" As soon as she walks out the door, reality will sink in, and she'll wonder what planet you're from and why she came to see you to begin with.

She'll immediately talk to her friends and pass on what hap-pened. Word of mouth is the quickest and most effective adver-tising method. In about eight minutes, everyone in the unit will know that you're not a good listener.

Here's a question that will bumfuzzle all the men reading this. (Hey, I know because I *am* one.) What's the first step in the lis-tening process? Nope. Try again. Men, it's *shut up*! Yeah, I know that hit you between the eyes. It *should* hit you between the ears. What's interesting is that the women get it on the first try! The truth is, we're scripted and trained to provide answers.

*Shut up* and *listen* are foreign terms to us men. No kidding! Say that to a guy and he'll say, "Huh?" But that's what you've got to do: *shut up, and listen for the question*! Again, it's often at the end of the dialogue. Maybe shutting down is the key. You have to shut down your own perspective to get the speaker's perspec-tive first. Then you can use the benefit of all your wisdom to in-spire the seeker to develop his or her own answer. Most people already have the answer to their problem by the time they come to see you. They just don't like the answer or want someone to validate it. The best you can do is let them choose their own solution. Often, all they need is someone to listen. Do that, and the word will get out that you're exceptional.

*Shutting up is the first critical part of the listening process; another is paying attention to nonverbal communication.* We often say more with our bodies than we do with our words. Tone of voice will tell you a lot about how people feel and what they want to communicate. Debbie, my lovely bride of 28 wonderful and fulfilling years, has exactly five ways she says my name. Two of them are good! Listen for feeling as well as content. That may take some skill, but you can develop it if you try. Take some listening courses if you can find them. Strive to listen empathically. That means don't judge what you're hearing—just accept it as the speaker's view. After people tell you what they want to tell you, then ask if they're looking for advice. You'll have to use your intuition here. Remember that they may say what they think you might want them to say. Listen with your eyes as well as your ears. If they say no, don't offer it. You've done your job. If they do want advice, make sure they understand that it's based on your limited experience and that the final decision is theirs alone. Keep in mind that they might say yes when you ask them if they want your advice only because they think you want to advise them. As you become a better listener, you'll develop a stronger trust. When that happens, your troops will feel better about telling you whether they truly want your advice or whether they just want you to listen. When they come for the latter, count it a success.

*One of the most important aspects of good listening is not interrupting.* Have you ever talked with people who finish your every sentence? If they know what you're going to say, why waste your time saying it? Those folks can carry on your conversation and theirs at the same time. As difficult as it may be, don't interrupt. My lovely bride calls it interactive listening. It's become a cultural thing, I think. It's un-American not to interrupt! Let the speaker finish. Wait for that punch line. Many American Indian cultures have a really neat listening process when they're in council. They have what they call a talking stick. The person who holds it gets to talk. Those who do not hold the stick get to shut up and listen. They say nothing at all until it's their turn for the stick. My baby sister gave me one of them for Christmas. I've had to adjust the process a little, though. I smack people with it every time they start to interrupt! (Hey, sometimes you do what you have to do! Okay, I don't do that, but I often consider it.) The point is, don't interrupt. It's rude, and you may miss the point if you do.

*Shut up! Shut down! Listen! Pay attention!* Be aware that once your troops know you're a good listener, they will seek you out.

11

Very few people know how to listen. The power in that skill is that you'll be trusted and you'll be able to help others. Listening will empower you to learn. And there is so much to learn, whether about people or the work you do. Listen and pay attention. Your troops will soon respect you for it. If you make it a habit to listen well, I guarantee you that you're on your way to becoming an Exceptionally Powerful Lieutenant!

## War Story

This story may seem out of context, but as you read it, you'll understand its value. Although it doesn't refer to how you deal with your troops directly, it has much to do with how we listen, what we listen for, and what effect our listening can have on others.

I'm sitting at the table on a Monday morning with all of the wing's group and unit commanders as the new general asks questions, trying to understand what his wing is about. "Why is that building across the street from the security forces building green when all the others on the base are beige?" he asks. Eyes in the headlights all around. Most of the commanders are new as well, so they don't know. No one responds with a plausible answer. The meeting goes on. I think nothing of it.

Later in the week, I make a point to explore the base a bit. Remembering the general's question, I go over to see that building he'd asked about. Sure enough, it's green—not beige like all the others around it. As I get closer, I notice a group of enlisted troops in front of the building. Even from a distance, I can tell they're in an animated conversation. As I walk up, I quickly get the gist of their discussion and ask the senior person what's going on. "We have to paint this building by the end of the day, Chief," the NOCIC tells me. "Why?" I ask, "It seems like the paint is still holding up." "Our commander said the general doesn't like the color, so we're going to paint it the same color as the others," he responds.

Snitch that I am, I immediately go back to headquarters and talk with the general. "Sir, did you tell anyone to paint that green building across from the security forces building?" "No, Chief, I didn't. Why do you ask?" "Because there's a group of

Airmen over there getting ready to do just that. And they've got plenty on their plate right now without having to be painters."

Needless to say, the general gets on the horn (that's a telephone for you young folks) and stops that tasking. So what, you say? Here's the listening lesson: that group's commander had read into the general's question much more than was there. As the general and I talked, he made it clear that his question was a sincere and naïve one. He just wondered why that building was a different color. The commander *assumed* (there's that word again) that the general didn't like it, and, being an overachiever (as many commanders are), he was trying to please his boss. He didn't shut up or shut down; instead, he started coming up with a solution for a problem that wasn't even a problem.

Do you think that the commander's overaggressiveness might have had an effect on the troops? A big one! They had other, much more important, duties to accomplish. That commander was more intent on doing what he thought his boss wanted than considering what was right in the larger scheme of things and doing that.

Listen. Pay attention. Make sure you understand the message. Don't assume—it makes an ass out of you and me. You probably don't need any help doing that!

## Starting Points

- Do I really want to understand, or do I just want to impress the speaker?

- Do I shut down to hear the speaker's message from his or her perspective, not mine?

- Am I observant of body language?

- When should I give advice?

## Words of Wisdom

*Courage is what it takes to stand up and speak; courage is also what it takes to sit down and listen.*

—Winston Churchill

13

*Generosity gives assistance rather than advice.*

—Marquis de Vauvenargues

*Hearing is one of the body's five senses. But listening is an art.*

—Frank Tyger

*He that would be a leader must be a bridge.*

—Welsh proverb

*Why is it always easier to dislike something than to understand it?*

—Unknown

*I have two ears so I can hear both sides of any argument.*

—Noah benShea

*It's not what we say that matters. It's what the other person hears.*

—Mort Crimm

*The ear of the leader must ring with the voices of the people.*

—Woodrow Wilson

Habit 3

# Look Up!
## Attitude Is Everything

"He's got an attitude!" Have you ever said that about some-one? Has anyone ever said that about *you*? (Okay, if you're a she, has anyone ever said, "She's got an attitude!" about you?) Chances are you're nodding your head or looking to see if people are around so they don't see you acknowledging the truth. *You've* got an attitude! Yes, you do. As I do. And mine is proba-bly bigger than yours. After all, I've got more to have an attitude about. The question is, What *kind* of attitude? In case I haven't said it yet, life is all about choices. You will choose—and express—either a positive attitude or a negative attitude. There is no in-between. You have to choose, so make the *right* choice. What's the right choice? Imagine the following:

"That person" comes in to the unit every day with a scowl on his face. Of course, we're talking about someone else. It's more convenient that way. This particular day the planets and stars align, showing you the answer to the most important issue you're working on at the unit. It's the one change that can make everything—and I mean everything—better for everyone. Hooah! When implemented, this idea will produce quantum progress. You happen to work for "that person," so you can hardly wait to go in to share this great thought with him. True to his normal attitude, he shoots down everything—and I mean everything—you say. He doesn't even hear you out (he doesn't know habit 2) before he starts ranting about how stupid an idea it is. I know that's never happened to you, but pretend it has.

Now imagine going through the same scenario with a boss who has read this book and is applying its tenets. After hearing your plan completely, without interrupting, she looks you in the eye and says, "Great idea! Let's see if we can make it work! It may not work exactly as you've envisioned it, but we can tweak it along the way until it works. We'll all be better for it. Great work, Lieutenant! Thanks!"

Okay, now choose. With whom would you prefer to work? Do you need any hints? Probably not. Do you think that the attitude a leader expresses will affect those whom he or she leads and works with? Man, you're so smart! His or her attitude will permeate everything. *Attitude is everything because it affects everything*—and I mean *everything*!

Let's see how smart you really are. Where do people's attitudes come from: (a) the way they were raised, (b) the responsibilities they have on their shoulders, (c) their DNA, or (d) the choices they make? You *are* smart! And growing smarter as you read, right?

The truth is that *attitude comes from the heart, works its way through the brain into the mouth, and comes out through the hands.* Kind of like the leg bone is connected to the knee bone. . . . (Ask some old*er* person to share that song with you.) Your heart is where you keep your purpose. Why are you doing what you're doing? If it's for money, forget it! You'll never make it rich in the lieutenant business. If it's to support your troops and help them grow, you're on your way to becoming an Exceptionally Powerful Lieutenant! Your most sincere intentions, however, can become misguided if you don't think about how to make them real to others—namely, those you lead. You have to think about their needs as well as how they communicate and then try to speak at their level, which may be higher than yours. Remember the old adage "Sticks and stones may break my bones, but words will never hurt me"? Isn't that *stupid*? Actually, sticks and stones may break our bones, but words will break our hearts and spirits. What we *do*, with the wrong attitude, can cause even more irreversible damage. Work on saying and doing the right thing at the right time in the right way for the right reason. You'd expect that from others, wouldn't you? *Your attitude is yours and yours alone.* Choose the right one. You *will* share it—like it or not.

Let me use an analogy I borrowed from Maj Dave Keller, a good friend and hero. What is this? Oh, right, you can't see that I'm holding an outdoor thermometer. Pretend you can see it. Again, what is this? Yes, that's right; it's a thermometer. What does a thermometer do? Okay. . . . Yes! It assesses the environment, doesn't it? You were pretty close. A thermometer tells you whether it's hot or cold or how hot or cold it is, right? It assesses the environment. Now what is this? Oh, sorry. Pretend you see the thermostat I'm holding. Yes, that's right; it's a thermostat. Now, what does *it* do? It *controls* the environment. Hooah! You're right on! Okay, don't get too technical; just go with me on this. (Some of you are *too* smart!) Now here's a choice question: would you prefer to be a thermometer, an instrument that assesses the environment, one that goes around telling everyone when life stinks; or would you rather be a thermostat, controlling those external things that bombard you and can influence you? Remember the two scenarios at the beginning of this lesson? Which of those two bosses was a thermometer? Which was a thermostat? Which are *you*?

Yeah, I know. Some of you are saying that's a faulty analogy. Blame Major Keller; he's the one who showed it to me! (Okay, I'm just kidding; my attitude started showing! Don't blame anyone.) Here's the deal: although a thermometer doesn't *always* say it stinks, it always takes its attitude from external sources. The thermostat controls those sources. You may think like Geraldine Jones, Flip Wilson's character, that "the devil made me do it!" (Okay, find that old*er* person who helped you with the knee-bone song and ask her to tell you who Flip Wilson is.) *Your attitude comes from you.* You may let external events influence it, but you will always have to make the choice. You choose your attitude and then share it with everyone around you. The sharing part is not a choice. You *will* share it with everyone around you because attitude is contagious. It affects everyone you touch. It even affects morale.

Let me talk about morale for a minute. We often think of morale in terms of the troops being happy. The troops are *never* happy! Okay, that's not true. Sometimes they are. They're happy when they have good leaders to follow. Being happy is not necessarily what morale is about though. It's about attitude! I've been in places like Bosnia, Turkey, and Saudi Arabia, where the troops weren't happy, but morale was high. I remember being in the mud, literally, in Bosnia working alongside soldiers who put their lives on the line every day. They certainly weren't happy, but morale was high due to their attitudes, which were positive because they realized that what they were doing had meaning. They had to do their jobs because their buddies' lives depended on it. They had a sense of purpose and mission. They refused to let external things keep them from performing their duties. They were thermostats! Every time I think of those men and women, my heart swells with pride. They were—and still are, I'm sure—warriors of honor! A big hooah to each of them! *Morale has to do with attitude. A positive attitude, especially from leaders, will filter through a unit and create high morale.* It always has. It always will.

Earlier I referred to an idea that would produce quantum progress. Chances are you understood that to mean huge progress, which is how most of us perceive the term *quantum*. The dictionary, however, defines it in terms of smallest, not largest. I used that term intentionally. Oftentimes the actions, the behaviors that have the greatest impact are the smallest and easiest to generate. That small thing you do creates big results, and those big results create small, high-impact behaviors. And then the cycle starts all over again, in a circle. Think about this: what very small, inexpensive act could you do daily that would produce a huge, positive impact on your troops? Something you can do every day with almost no effort but will make you a much stronger leader? An action or behavior that will create a positive attitude because it *comes* from a positive attitude? I won't lead you on too long. This is not *American Idol.* Simply saying "good morning" to your troops—and meaning it, of course—will reap *huge* benefits! I'll explain why in a second. What would that cost you? How much effort would it really take? Very little. What effect would it have on your troops? A quantum effect! Quantum in the sense that such a small investment can affect everyone in the unit and beyond. (I'm beginning to sound like Buzz Lightyear in *Toy Story 2*, aren't I? You may need a young*er* person to help you with that movie.)

It's the little things you do that express your attitude. Here's why those small acts produce such large benefits. Everyone wants to feel valued. Even lieutenants. When you acknowledge a person's presence (or is it *presents*?), you're telling that person you care. (The next habit focuses on caring, so I won't elaborate here.) Every person in our military forces is valuable. Exceptionally Powerful Lieutenants will ensure that all of their troops know that they're valued every day. Wishing your troops a good morning and acknowledging their presence is a very small price to pay for the return you'll get. Add a smile, and they will say great things about you. In fact, a sincere smile and respect-ful greeting will say much more about your attitude than all the speeches you can ever deliver. (For those of you who work dif-ferent shifts, you'll have to say the appropriate words, but I think you catch my drift, don't you?)

When I was young (I was, many years ago), my mom and dad would always wish my siblings and me a good morning and ask how we slept. That may be a cultural thing; I don't know. First, they wanted to welcome us to another wonderful day. Second, they were sincerely interested that we'd had a good night's sleep. That was a great start to every day! We didn't have much grow-ing up in materialistic terms, but we had all we needed in atti-tude. That's where "Isn't this a great day?" started.

I often hear people tell me, "Well, I'm not a morning person." Get over it! I think that's a cop-out for choosing a negative atti-tude. Imagine the power of developing a habit that puts you in a positive frame of mind at the start of the day. Do you think it might carry on the rest of the day? Do you think it might affect the people you lead? Try it, and then answer those questions. Try what? Think about the next couple of paragraphs.

Although I chose "Attitude Is Everything" as the subtitle for this habit, the title is "Look Up!" Keith D. Harrell, author of *Atti-tude Is Everything*, has a new book called *An Attitude of Grati-tude*. I'm a self-acknowledged hypocrite, so I'd like to practice that now. Although attitude is everything, gratitude is more. (Okay, I'm going in circles. I like circles, especially when I'm in the right ones.) Here's how I see it (and it *is* a circle). Your atti-tude will come from a sense of gratitude that will affect your attitude. If you're truly grateful for what you have, your attitude will reflect that. And it will affect everyone around you.

The mother of Zig Ziglar, a motivational speaker, says, "When the outlook isn't good, try the up-look." In other words, look up. Search for meaning beyond you and above you. Your attitude will reflect your hope. Hope is a very powerful concept, particularly when you're leading troops. Your business is war, whether you like it or not. As a leader, your troops will often look up to you to gain their hope. When you provide it to them, they will excel be-cause their attitude will be positive. Hope is like faith. You can't hold it in your hands, but you know when you have it and when you don't. Your troops do too! It's interesting that we find hope in ourselves by having faith in something larger than we can possibly be. Find faith and hope, and let them raise your attitude so that every one of your troops will say, "I'll go to war with that Exceptionally Powerful Lieutenant! Any day! Any place!"

Maj Chappy Watties, my pastor and good friend, and I were sitting in Bosnia waiting for a plane to take us back to Germany. We're both philosophers although he's much wiser than I. As we were sitting there analyzing the world around us, he told me, "Chief, there are two types of people in this world. Those who get up in the morning and say, 'Good morning, God!' and those who get up in the morning and say, 'Good God, morning!'" Again, it's your choice. Attitude is contagious, and your troops will catch it from you. You choose.

Be a thermostat! *Choose a positive attitude*! Be thankful for what you have. Share that gratitude with your troops. Stand beside them, and help them look up and aim high.

## War Story

I'm at the Brandenburg Gate one cold and dreary October morning in Berlin, Germany. (Okay, almost every morning is cold and dreary in Berlin. So what's new?) I'm sitting in a bus full of enlisted Air Force bandsmen waiting to march in the first-ever Unification Day Parade. I'm serving as the drum major for the United States Air Forces in Europe (USAFE) Band. The troops are restless. They're cold, and it's raining. You can probably understand how they feel only if you've been there. As troops sometimes do, they start to get rowdy. Some are "tough" enough to approach me and ask whether we can cancel our march because "the cold, wet weather can negatively affect our instruments and our uniforms, which would cost a lot of money to replace." Any warrior would know the answer. Let me say that these are real warriors. It's just that after being out all night in Berlin (acting as American ambassadors of goodwill, of course), it's very difficult to think clearly first thing in the morning.

Anyway, being the astute student of group dynamics that I am, I stand up and start trying to inspire the troops by telling them how important this parade is, politically and emotionally, not only to the German population but also to the United States government. I was *on*, man! I could see morale growing with my every word. I finished my short yet very eloquent speech by saying, "It could be worse. It could be snowing!" As I said that, their eyes changed as they looked beyond me. Someone pointed. I turned around to see that it *was* snowing. We still marched in the parade.

My point is that regardless of how tough things get, they could always be worse. If they're not worse, be grateful for it. By the way, if you'd like to see a picture of that parade, go to the USAFE Band's Web site. You have to look hard to see me since I'm facing the band, but you can see the cold, wet troops marching proudly in front of the Brandenburg Gate. They represented you well—after they adjusted their attitudes.

## Starting Points

- Isn't this a *great* day to be an American warrior?
- Have I acknowledged my troops' "presents" today?
- What am I truly grateful for?
- Am I being a thermostat today?

## Words of Wisdom

*A little spark kindles a great fire.*

—Spanish proverb

*Growth in wisdom may be exactly measured by decrease in bitterness.*

—Friedrich Nietzsche

*All I have seen teaches me to trust the Creator for all I have not seen.*

—Ralph Waldo Emerson

*That man is happiest who lives from day to day and asks no more, garnering the simple goodness of life.*

—Euripides

21

*He is rich that is satisfied.*

—Thomas Fuller

*The world is wide, and I will not waste my life in friction when it could be turned into momentum.*

—Frances Willard

*There are moments when everything goes well, but don't be frightened.*

—Jules Renard

*A successful man is one who can lay a firm foundation with the bricks others have thrown at him.*

—David Brinkley

# Be Care-Full!
## Take Care of Your Troops

Man, I loved that guy! Well, actually, I still do. I worked with a general officer with whom I would still go to war without hesitation. If he called me this very minute and said, "Chief, I need you to go to Timbuktu with me," my only question would be, "When do you need me to be there, General?" I'd even accept his collect call! As much as I truly found it an honor to serve with him, he also frustrated the dickens out of me. He was never—and I mean never—on time. His wife is laughing her head off as she reads this because she knows how bad he was about being late. She often said, "He'll be late for his own funeral."

Let me tell you that he never intended to be late. Oftentimes, he got so deep in discussion with people, trying to help them out, that he'd forget he had another appointment. Remember I told you this: when you become a general officer, you will continuously run from one appointment to the next. Unintentionally, the message my general sent to those whom he kept waiting was that he didn't respect their time. As hard as I tried to explain to audiences that he meant no disrespect, that's how they often took it. Know this: what you intend doesn't matter nearly as much as how others perceive your behavior. Perception is truth to the perceiver. If those you lead think you don't respect them, you'd better change your behavior because it's the only thing that will change their minds.

Leadership guru John Maxwell says that followers have to buy into leaders before they buy into their vision. I believe that's true. How do leaders get people to buy into them? They have to show that they care. How can *you* show that you care? More on that in a minute. You may have heard the adage "People don't care how much you know until they know how much you care." The hard truth is that people *do* know how much you care by your attitude and what you're willing to do to help them empower themselves. If you care for them and treat them like winners, they'll live up to your expectations. On the other hand, if you treat them like dirtbags, they'll live up to your expectations.

*Caring is about the little things you do, or don't do, that express your concern for your troops—or your family, for that matter.* (Don't worry, I'll write a book on Exceptionally Powerful Families.) I mentioned the little things in the last habit. To be care-full means you have to be full of care. The subtitle of this habit, "Take Care of Your Troops," is critical to your success. Exceptionally Powerful Lieutenants will *show* their troops that they care. You'll expect your troops to be on time, won't you? It's a matter of respect, isn't it? Here's the most powerful lesson in this book: *to gain respect, you must give it.* That's the *only* way you'll gain it. Trust me! What you give, you will get in return. That's the way of the world. If you respect your troops enough to be on time, they will do the same. Interestingly, one of the biggest issues we dealt with in that wing led by my general was on-time takeoffs. Could there have been a correlation? You decide.

One of the most difficult things you will learn as a leader is that the cliché "It's lonely at the top" is true. So bring someone with you! If you expect to be an Exceptionally Powerful Lieutenant, you'll have to be care-full. You will also have to be careful not to get too close to the troops. "Wait a minute," you say, "first you tell me to take care of them, but now you're telling me to be careful of them. What's up with that?" Here's what I mean.

Who is accountable for the welfare of the troops and the accomplishment of the mission? You guessed it. It's you. Do you think that those two elements may come into conflict at any time? Man, you're smart! Surely, you've heard the old adage "Take care of your troops, and they will take care of the mission." That statement is also true. Taking care of the troops has much to do with nurturing an environment conducive to growth. Being care-full means holding your troops accountable so that they can grow and mature into better leaders themselves. How you do that is critical to your success as a leader. It often requires a different approach for every person you lead. When he was commander of USAFE, Gen John Jumper used a term that captures what I'm getting at. The term was *tough love*. I'm not sure who found it tough when it came to holding people accountable. Let me go back to my general for an example.

He was the best leader I ever worked with. His expectations were high, but I always knew what they were. When he first took command, he sent out printed pamphlets of what he expected from his wing. He was easy to follow because we all knew what he expected. Anyway, I recall that he asked me (you don't really order chiefs) to do something. I agreed and went out to do it. Some time later, I had to come back to him to tell him that I had failed (yes, yes, even chiefs fail—but only once). I felt terrible that I hadn't been able to accomplish what he'd asked me to do. Evidently, he saw my frustration. After I explained to him what had happened—or hadn't happened—he looked me in the eye and said, "It won't happen again, will it, Chief?" Of course, my answer was, "No, Sir!" "Thanks!" he said. I'm sitting there, waiting to be admonished. Yell at me, man! Hit me! Do something! He just said, "Thank you" and dismissed me. That was the toughest admonishment I'd ever gotten. You see, he knew I didn't need any more than that. He knew I'd kick my own butt better than he could. Do you see why I'd go to war with that man any day, any place?

*The point is that you have to know how to take care of your troops in a way that will help them grow and fulfill the mission.* You have to be flexible in how you do that because your troops will respond differently to everything that happens to them in their lives. There is no "cookie-cutter" method for leading people. You have to show them you care, but at the same time you must separate yourself from them enough to be able to do what you need to do. That takes discipline. All of this sounds confusing, doesn't it?

*Discipline* is a word that we often use in a negative way. You can do that, and you'll get negative results. You'll think they're positive results because you may see immediate changes, but in the long term they will be negative. Let me explain. Here's one of several definitions of *discipline*: punishment intended to correct or train. Now is *punishment* a word that will get you positive results? If you answer yes, call me. You need help. We think of discipline as punishment, and it can certainly be that if you so choose. But the root word of *discipline* is *disciple*—one who embraces and assists in spreading the teachings of another. Now we're getting into a positive tone, aren't we? Effective discipline comes from caring. Have you ever been to a gathering where promotions were announced? Remember the reactions of the troops when their new leader was introduced? "Ladies and gentlemen," the emcee announces, "I give you your new leader, Lt Bag O. Donuts!" The troops say nothing. The hush is deafening. Do you think there was much discipline or discipleship in that unit? I don't think so. On the other hand, consider this scenario: "Ladies and gentlemen, I give you your new leader, the Exceptionally Powerful Lieutenant Jones!" The place goes crazy. The troops hooah themselves hoarse! They are ready and willing to follow that lieutenant to war right now! Hooah, Lieutenant! What's the difference? The Exceptionally Powerful Lieutenant Jones takes care of her troops. She's care-full.

So how will you take care of your troops? If you'll recall, in habit 3, "Look Up!" we talked about the power of saying "good morning." That's one of the little things that produces big results. Let me give you four other parts of this puzzle.

*First, tell them what you expect.* Remember, I just told you I respected my general so much because I knew what he expected of me. Most leaders assume that their followers know what they expect. Often, they hold their followers accountable for doing what they assumed their followers knew was expected of them but never told them. Is that confusing or what? Try being in the middle of all that! I've been there, and it wasn't fun.

The most powerful process I've found that will produce quantum positive results in dealing with expectations comes from Covey's book *The 7 Habits of Highly Effective People.* He calls it the win-win agreement, which includes five general areas: desired results (what you expect), resources (what you have to work with), guidelines (rules of engagement), accountability (who's responsible for what), and consequences (what happens after success or failure). Key to that process is agreement. Both you and your troops agree to live up to the expectations in each area. When you both agree, that breeds discipline or discipleship for both parties. Another critical concept is to let your troops be creative. They have all kinds of ideas, so let them loose to share them with you. The win-win agreement process takes time, but the investment will bring huge returns.

*Second, know your troops.* I didn't say go drink with them! Observe them. Listen to them. You know what that takes after having mastered habit 2. Listen. Pay attention. Try to analyze their needs. Now, I'm not asking you to turn into a psychologist or anything like that. Just watch and learn. What are they interested in? How can you help them grow? Think of them as winners, and help them reach the finish line first. They will love you and follow you anywhere!

Here's an important lesson. This one's free: your troops, with very few exceptions, will value their families more than anything else. Learn as much as you can about their families and how you can help them invest more time with their loved ones. I know that may not be easy, but if you're interested—really care-full—they will appreciate and remember anything you do for them in that area of their lives. You see, taking care of work issues is easy compared to dealing with family issues. As the saying goes, "If Momma ain't happy, ain't nobody happy." If your troops are having family problems, they won't give you 100 percent at work. That's just how life is. So do what you can, even if it's not a lot, to help your troops take care of their families. If you do, they will go to war with you any day, any place.

*Third, humble yourself.* Yeah, you're the lieutenant. At least in your mind, you're the boss. Get over it! You're still accountable, but you're not going to succeed unless your troops become your disciples. If you're cocky and try to impress them with your authority, you'll quickly find how lonely it can be at the top. I can remember getting so much more done than I was capable of doing only because I could humble myself and ask young troops for help. "Man, the chief needs *me*? I'm there for him!" they would say in their hearts. I'd then get out of the way and let them excel. I always gave them credit for their work when I got credit for the accomplishment.

Never ask your troops to do more than you're willing to do. Lt Hank Emerson was one of the best men I ever worked with. He was young and eager to be a good leader. He had one problem, though. He never asked his troops to do more than he was willing to do. Well, his problem was that he often did it for them! I remember the old chiefs admonishing him to let the troops do what they were supposed to do, what they were hired to do. Bless his heart; the lieutenant cared so much that he wanted to do their work for them and spare them the trouble. At the beginning of this paragraph I said, "Never ask your troops to do more than you're willing to do." The lesson is, Don't do it unless they need your help. If you're the only officer in the unit, your loneliness may try to overtake you. Your troops need to know that you're the leader. It's very difficult to lead from the trenches. As a new leader, you don't have enough experience to do that effectively. Be willing to help and get your hands dirty if you're needed, but don't make that a habit. Immature folks will try to take advantage of it, and you don't need that bombarding you. I hope this makes sense. It's a paradox, I know, but it's true.

Humility is not the easiest virtue to embody. It takes a great deal of internal strength and a sense of purpose. If you're there to take care of your troops so that they can take care of the mission, you will excel because you will humble yourself to your purpose. If you're there to get promoted, watch out! Your troops will sense that in eight seconds and will make life hell for you. I believe it was Ken Blanchard who said, "Humble people don't think less of themselves; they think of themselves less."

Let me put it this way. You graduated from high school. For four or five years, you went to an academy or college where they taught you to be a "leader." You may have some type of technical training. You're all of 22 years old. You get to your first assignment where you're put in charge of an E-9 who's been in service 30 years! Do you think you might get a very quick lesson in humility from that E-9? Twenty-two years old! Man, I've got socks older than you! In fact, I'm wearing them right now. That's just the E-9. All the other troops you're now in charge of have been to war more times than you've been to the bathroom! (Okay, that's probably an exaggeration, but you know what I mean.) How are you going to lead those people? By following. By being humble. You'll learn more about that when you get to habit 8. *Humility is key to being an Exceptionally Powerful Lieutenant.*

*Last, be consistent in your attitude and behavior.* According to Don Shula and Ken Blanchard, "Consistency is not behaving the same way all the time: it is behaving the same way in similar circumstances." I've always preferred to work with leaders who were consistent. I could always count on how they would respond to what I did. Even those who were consistently negative were easier to work with than those who kept me guessing. My sense is that those who kept me guessing had no clear sense of purpose, nor did they practice humility. You should know by now that I would never advocate negative behavior of any type.

So be consistently positive, and you will get consistently positive results. That's how life works! I guess that goes back to habit 3 and having a positive attitude, doesn't it? You'll find that all of these habits intertwine to make you a total-person leader.

Chief Seattle of the Suquamish and Duwamish Native American tribes said in 1854 that "all things are connected. Whatever befalls the earth befalls the sons of the earth. Man did not weave the web of life: he is merely a strand in it. Whatever he does to the web, he does to himself." Those words tell me that what we do on a daily basis affects our world in profound ways, so the best thing we can do is understand that the people around us are more important than we are. The most exceptionally power-ful people are humble. Humility is about being care-full—putting others first. When we do, others will put us first. It's the circle of life. I used to tell newcomers to my unit that they had to follow two rules: (1) take care of the chief, and (2) the chief will take care of you. In truth, those rules worked backward, but they didn't have to know that. If you take care of the troops, they will take care of the mission, and they will take care of you. They *will* know how much you care by what you say, what you think, what you do, and how you do it—so be care-full!

## War Story

My lovely bride of 28 wonderful and fulfilling years (the number increases each year, by the way) and I were married on 28 January 1978 (please feel free to send gifts on that day—or any other day, for that matter). By the end of February of that year, I was at Clark Air Base (AB) in the Philippines. We hadn't had time to get her passport, so she had to stay home in Charlotte, North Carolina, with her parents until she got her documents. I did all I could to expedite the process, but I was a young staff sergeant at the time and rather naïve about how things worked, so I wasn't very successful.

Hold on. Let me go back a little. In November of 1977, my mom contracted Guillain-Barré syndrome, a type of polio that almost killed her, hospitalizing her for many months. I found out about Mom's illness just after I'd gotten orders for reassignment to the Air Force Band of the Pacific at Clark AB. Because I had a report date of February 1978, I immediately asked that it be changed so I could be sure of her recovery before I went "across the pond," as we old guys say. My gaining-unit commander denied the request because I was needed on a band tour since I was the only bassoonist.

Good warrior that I was, I left my mom in the hospital and my bride at home awaiting a passport and proceeded to my new duty station in the Philippines. After I made all kinds of calls and asked everyone I knew, including my commander, for help (who, by the way, never did), Mom got out of the hospital and Deb got her papers. I was relieved that Mom survived, although she has never been able to walk since, and excited that Deb could join me. I worked hard to make arrangements for her to fly to Clark, but I ran into a glitch. The only available flights would arrive during the time we would be on the tour for which I was so desperately needed. During the negotiations for changing my arrival date, the commander had fixed the band orchestrations so that another instrument covered my parts—as a precaution, I suppose. In other words, I really wasn't needed on that tour anymore. You can imagine how I felt having left Mom in the hospital so that I could do my duty, which, in the end, wasn't critical.

Under the circumstances, I asked to be left behind so that I could pick up my new bride at the airport and set up our household—you know, all the typical things that have to be done when you get to a new assignment. The answer, to my surprise, was no! I had to go on the tour. I went and didn't do much—but I was there. Deb had to wait another month to join me. Again, can you imagine how I felt? Do you think I was a gung-ho warrior at that time?

I'm not bitter now, but I was then. Why? My commander was not care-full. I never got to talk with him. The E-9 we had in the unit was the only person who gave me an audience—but he didn't care either. I never understood why they had made their decisions, and they never tried to explain them. I suppose they didn't have to, but they certainly would have gotten more out of me if they had.

One of the good things about military life is that everything changes when a new commander comes in, every two years or so. Or does it? The commander and E-9 who had no idea how to be care-full were reassigned, and two new people took command. "Hooah!" I thought. I'll admit they were more care-full than the previous regime, but something happened that I hope you will never allow, although I see it in units to this day. You have to stop it! Let me explain.

As I said earlier, I was a naïve staff sergeant just doing my job. But I was a hard worker, so I deserved to be promoted. And I got promoted although I almost didn't know it. Here's what happened. Deb and I were at the park in the housing compound where we lived. For some reason, ironically, I hadn't gone on this particular band tour. The band had just returned, and at the park I happened to see the E-8 (the one who had replaced the previous E-9) since he lived in our housing area. After the usual salutations he said,

"By the way, congratulations!"

"Congratulations? On what?"

"On your promotion."

"What promotion?"

"To tech sergeant. Didn't anyone tell you?"

Obviously, the answer was no. No one had told me. Deb and I should have been jumping for joy, I suppose, since it *was* good news. We were more confused than elated, though. That was not exactly the best way to learn about a promotion.

There are two lessons here. First, as I said before, your troops' families will almost always be the highest priority in their lives. If you help them take care of their families, they will do anything you ask of them and more. I certainly would have been more productive at that Philippines assignment if I'd trusted my leaders to take care of my family. In truth, you would have had to shoot *me* to go to war voluntarily with any of those men.

Second, you'll have to do some unpleasant things in your duty as a commander—too many of them. One of the few *good* things you'll do is promote your troops. That should be a momentous event. When your troops get promoted, find them—no matter where they are—and present them their new stripes. If they have family and you can include them, do it! Promotion is the acknowledgement of value. We all want to be valued. I know you've heard that before. The small things you do every day to express how you value your troops are incredibly powerful. But a promotion is the institution's formal way of expressing its respect and trust in a warrior. It should be an unforgettable event—a positive, unforgettable event. I guarantee you that we all remember every one of our promotions. And we remember who was in command. If you're care-full, you'll spend less time being careful because you'll have a team of experienced, knowledgeable, caring warriors around you doing all they can to help you become an Exceptionally Powerful Lieutenant!

## Bonus War Story

As I put the finishing touches on this book, something happened that led me to add this story. Ronald Reagan, former president of the United States, passed away. Put political differences aside for a minute, and listen to this because I think it further validates my point about being care-full.

As I previously mentioned, I served in several Air Force bands (most, unfortunately, don't exist anymore). While serving with the Air Force Band of the Golden West, stationed at March AFB in California, we had many opportunities to play for President Reagan at various high-level events. Evidently, he liked us because after he retired to the Los Angeles area, he called us to come visit him so that he could thank us for what we'd done for him while he was in office. Now, think on that a little bit—a former president of the United States summoning members of an Air Force band to his office to thank them! That in itself is being care-full. He didn't have to do it. But he did!

We took advantage of the invitation and went to his office one bright, sunny day. (It's always bright and sunny in California.) What an exciting time! The president invested more than an hour with us, joking around and telling stories. What a great storyteller! We all had our pictures taken with him. (I have mine proudly displayed in my office if you'd like to come by and see it.) Apparently, his next appointment was some golf tournament. He was dressed casually since he had to go to the course right after talking with us. I was the second-to-last person to be photographed with him. My commander was last. I'd trained him. As we finished taking the photos, one of the president's aides came in and admonished him that he needed to hurry to get to his next commitment. The president acknowledged the remark but finished the photos. Again, he could have apologized and rushed off with his aide, but he stayed with us until we were all done.

I had brought my copy of *An American Life*, the president's autobiography, to be autographed. We hadn't had time for that, however, so as we were being led out of his office, I asked another aide at a desk near the door if she would please ask the president to autograph my book and I would gladly leave enough money with her to cover the postage to mail it to me. Although President Reagan was being escorted out another door, he stopped, having overheard my conversation. He told the aide with him to get my book, signed it, had his aide return it to me, and then went on his way. Did he have to do that? Of course not. But he did! He cared enough to stop what he was doing to take care of someone he didn't know very well but respected. He even remembered my name and, most importantly, my rank. He signed it

To Chief Bob Vásquez—With Best Wishes

Ronald Reagan

May 17 '93

You're welcome to come see my book as well. I won't let you touch it, but you can see it.

Many people loved President Reagan. Even more respected him. Surely, history will remember what he did for the country, but the people he touched will always remember him for how he treated them. He was care-full. I would have gone to war with him any time, any place. God bless you, Mr. President!

## Starting Points

- What do I know about my troops' families?
- Do my troops know what I expect of them?
- Do I practice humility?
- Am I taking care of my troops, or am I just saying it?

## Words of Wisdom

*There are two ways of exerting one's strength: pushing down or pulling up.*

—Booker T. Washington

*The greatest carver does the least cutting.*

—Tao Te Ching

*Always do your best. What you plant now, you will harvest later.*

—Og Mandino

*It's important that people know what you stand for. It's equally important that they know what you won't stand for.*

—Mary H. Waldrip

*People will sit up and take notice of you if you will sit up and take notice of what makes them sit up and take notice.*

—Frank Romer

*We shall never know all the good that a simple smile can do.*

—Mother Teresa

*A desk is a dangerous place from which to watch the world.*

—John LeCarré

*Never tell people how to do things. Tell them what to do and they'll surprise you with their ingenuity.*

—Gen George S. Patton

Habit 5

# Sharpen the Sword!
## Take Care of Yourself First

A lieutenant is a leader. A lieutenant leads warriors. A lieutenant *is* a warrior! We use the term *warrior* extensively in the military, but what exactly *is* a warrior? A typical dictionary definition of the word is "one engaged or experienced in battle." I'm not sure how much *experience* you have in battle, but you're certainly *engaged* in one. Before you start hooahing, let me ask you this: where is the greatest battle in your life? Is it not inside you? Isn't making yourself do what you should do a continuous battle? If it's not, you're really the exception. We'll have you canonized as soon as you die. The biggest battle most of us will ever fight is the internal one. Joseph Campbell, American writer on mythology and comparative religion, talked about the "dragon within" when he referred to a person's daily internal struggles. What would it take to slay that dragon within? Wouldn't it help to have a sharp sword? Where do you find that weapon? The sword is within you. I'll soon tell you how to keep it sharpened.

First, let me ask you a few more questions. Have you ever known someone who seemed tired all the time? Maybe that person was someone you avoided because he or she was always moody and hard to get along with. Have you ever heard of someone who was on the fast track to success but burned out instead? A better question might be, Are *you* that someone? If you have ever suffered burnout, you need to develop and hone the habit I discuss here—and you need to start now!

In habit 4 I told you about the value of selflessness: the importance of serving others by being care-full. So you might think I'm being duplicitous when I tell you to make a habit of taking care of yourself first. This notion may go against every leadership lesson you've ever learned, but it's the truth. I would never lie to you. (Okay, unless it was for your own good.)

Here's the deal. Although serving others is key to being an effective leader, truthfully, what good are you if you're not around?

How effective are you when you're ill? Can you "hang" with the troops when you're worn out? Do they perceive you as an effective leader when you're not in tune with what's happening in your environment or your specialty? When you're having a bad day, does it affect those around you? How inspiring can you be when you're not inspired yourself?

Surely you've taken a flight on a commercial airline. During the safety briefing, the flight attendant will get to the part about the little yellow oxygen cup coming down in front of you in case the plane loses altitude quickly. The attendant's message is to don the mask *first*, take care of your kids, and then breathe normally. Breathe normally. Yeah, right! If that little yellow cup comes down in front of me, my first reaction will be to breathe as fast as I can—it's somehow associated with Abraham Maslow's hierarchy of needs. Survival is the first need!

Now assuming I even remember that my wife and kids are with me on that flight, I'll certainly make sure they have their masks on too. My gut tells me that this is an especially difficult concept for moms. Dads are from the old school: "I brought you into this life, and I'll take you out!" More on that later. Moms will sacrifice *everything* for their children. Men think, "Hey, we'll just have more." (Okay, not really. Okay, maybe.) Anyway, the idea of taking care of yourself first is credible in this situation. It probably won't take you long to don the mask. If that's the only way to breathe, you'll do it with incredible speed. Rather than encouraging us to breathe normally, I think that the attendant really wants to keep us from panicking. That's one of the vital things you learn in CPR classes—don't panic. Emotional minds cause panic. Once it takes over, you can't think logically, and the fight-or-flight instinct assumes control—not a good thing. If you take care of yourself and don't panic, doesn't it make sense that you'll be able to assess what's going on a little bit better and make the right decisions? Then you'll be able to take care of others. I think so. Serving others begins with serving yourself.

*Your life includes four basic areas: physical, mental, emotional, and spiritual.* If you're going to serve others, you have to be healthy in those areas. Again, take care of yourself first, and then you can serve others. Let me break it down for you.

First, let's talk about *physical fitness*. How important is it? Of course, you know you have to take care of your body as long as you're in it. When you're not in it any more, don't worry about it. For several years now, Americans have been on a health kick. Still, we have ungodly numbers of people dying from heart attacks and strokes. The number of obese people increases continuously. Something's not right there, don't you think? Perhaps it's the New Year Resolution syndrome. Have you ever noticed that you can hardly get into the gym during the months of January, February, and March? By April you can walk in any time because it's almost empty. My biggest problem with maintaining physical fitness isn't so much that I don't have a program; it's that I won't stick with it consistently.

Is physical fitness important to taking care of yourself? Of course it is. What does it consist of? Most of us quickly develop the vision of looking like rapper LL Cool J or singer Jessica Simpson. (LL for the men and Jessica for the women, of course.) That's okay if you have the time and can make the commitment to it. But do you know what it takes to look like that? A lot of work! Most of us aren't willing to make that investment, but we still want those results. It won't happen! But you *can* maintain your health and even retain your girlish figure if you work at it consistently.

For years, physical fitness experts have told us that maintaining our hearts in good working condition requires only 20 minutes of aerobic exercise a day, three times a week. Twenty minutes, three times a week. If my ciphering is correct, that's one hour—per week. Do you know how many hours there are in a week? One hundred sixty-eight. (Trust me, I did the math.) Is it worth investing 1/168th of your time to increase your life span? If it increased by only one day, would it not be worth it? Well, yeah, but. . . .

Now get off your "buts." "But I don't have time!" "But I can't!" "But my shoes are too old!" Which "but" do you normally prefer? I'm not talking about lifting hundreds of pounds at the gym, but if that's what cranks your motor, great—do it! All I'm talking about, at a minimum, is taking a brisk walk for 20 minutes. Imagine! You're behind that computer you love, replying to every single e-mail for hours on end. Wouldn't it be nice to get up and take a walk for 20 minutes? If you did that twice a day, wouldn't you feel better and possibly increase your life span? Simple stuff! All you need is a place to do it (outdoors is great, but the mall will work too) and a pair of walking shoes. Part of our problem, I think, is that we want to look cool while we're exercising, and that becomes the priority. (I have a whole chapter on that. You'll have to wait for the next book.) You don't have to look cool to be healthy. That will come later when you *are* healthy!

The other part of physical fitness has to do with diet. I'll tell you now, this is the most difficult area of *my* life. I'd rather work out an hour a day, every day, than to give up the foods I like. I suppose it's better to strike a balance, whatever that is. (A balanced diet is *not* a Big Mac in each hand!) Again, you know the importance of not eating too much fat, eating whole grains, and drinking plenty of water. But I'm not an expert by any means. Get a good book that will help you eat sensibly—and not too much. I can't tell you how many times we Air Force bandsmen would go to a performance site after we'd had dinner only to find food set up for us. Although we'd just eaten, this food was *free*, man! Kids in Africa are starving, so how could we possibly waste free food? Luckily, most of our concerts were of a lighter vein. (Hey, I'm trying to keep you awake here!) The point is that diet is critical to physical fitness. Learn that before you have a heart attack, and you'll be much better off.

Another part of physical fitness has to do with the amount of rest we get regularly. I remember a TV commercial which professed that "the best never rest!" Yeah, well, they die young. The body is not constructed to work 24/7. We often think we can work that hard, but it ain't so! It needs to replenish its resources. Myriad studies conclude that if a person doesn't get enough rest, he or she will break down psychologically as well as physically. I know there's not enough time to do all you're asked to do, but if you don't rest, you'll eventually do nothing for a lot longer. Get plenty of rest, and make sure your troops do the same—or else! The "or else" will manifest itself in illness, weakness, and fatigue, all of which can compromise the mission. You know it's true.

Second, let's consider *the mental area of your life.* Let me add that maintaining physical fitness has an effect on our mental well-being. I recall that for most of my military life I was told, "We don't pay you to think; we pay you to do." Maybe, 100 years ago (20 in military years), that might have been the case. Now, with technology changing our world every day, you and your troops *have* to think. Our military suffers in two areas: not thinking and, when we do, what we think about.

Imagine walking down the hallway of your duty section only to find a young troop sitting there, doing nothing. I mean, he's just sitting there! *Doing nothing!* Ha! I'm a lieutenant! I'll fix that! "Young man, if you have nothing to do, let me find you something!" you say. Hey, I've been there, done that! You feel much better, don't you? Well, maybe you shouldn't. Is it possible that that young person was *thinking*? Is it possible that he or she was *this* close to coming up with a better way to perform your mission? Is it possible? You'll never know now, will you? How is it that we improve anything in our lives? Is it not through thinking? Someone, not you, thinks of a better way. Usually, it happens on the fly. Imagine if you and your troops made time to think of new ways to do things!

Regarding what you think about, I tell you, if you don't get your troops to sit down and think about something specific, they'll think about everything else. Have you ever asked one of your troops or yourself, "What *were* you thinking?" It's usually after they—or you—do something wrong that you ask that question. You *do* pay your troops to think! And you have to train them to do so!

So how do you exercise the mind? There are plenty of ways, but if you can't think of any, I have some suggestions: reading, for one. Leaders are readers. The problem with reading is that it takes time. None of us has time to read. We have to make time! You make time for watching *Survivor*, don't you? As with physical fitness, I'm not suggesting that you read *War and Peace*. Make 20 minutes available each day to read books about your favorite subjects, hobbies, or work. You might find some peace of mind. You might even learn something. The more you do it, the better you'll get at it. Read and learn. As you do it, your troops will see you and know that you value learning.

Hone your skills. More on that in the next habit, but suffice it to say that you can always find interesting classes to attend. Oh, I know, you're always on the road, the ops tempo is a killer, and the dog eats your homework. What do you produce when you rationalize? Rational lies! Get over it! As Hannibal said to his troops, "We shall find a way or make one!" (Or something like that. Hey, I wasn't there!) My point is that we have the means to do most anything nowadays. Technology connects us with people around the world. If you want to learn more about your profession, you can find a way to do so. Continue to learn.

Listening is an inexpensive way of exercising the mind. I already taught you how. Now practice it. Knowing but not doing is not knowing. Take what you read about in habit 2, and practice it daily. You may be amazed at what you can learn when you listen. Take that learning, and use it to accomplish your mission of either doing your job better or taking care of your troops better. You'll improve your mental health as well as the health of your troops. I'm going to sound duplicitous again, but when you take care of the troops, they'll take care of you! Don't waste your brain. Feed it daily.

Third, *you must hone your emotional life if you're going to lead anyone.* The first person you lead is you. I barely recall, about two centuries ago, the movie *The Greatest*, about Muhammad Ali—not the new version starring Will Smith, but the "real" one. The lyrics of the theme song, "Greatest Love of All," later recorded by Whitney Houston, referred to the greatest love of all as the love for oneself. At the time I thought, "How selfish!" As I matured (not aged), I came to realize that loving oneself *is* the first step to emotional stability. One cannot give what one does not have. (Wow, I hope I just made that up!) If you don't love yourself, how can you love anyone else? It's impossible! Life is about relationships. We often work on developing relationships with others. We also have to maintain a relationship with ourselves.

I hope you never have the experience of being around someone who's suicidal. When you become a commander, you'll probably have to deal with this situation in some way. Suicidal people have absolutely no love for themselves, and they will bring everyone around them down emotionally. You've been to those suicide-prevention briefings every year. But they never get to the real cause: the lack of self-love. The only way to help those who don't love themselves is to love them until they do. That's not easy, but it's the truth.

Now, don't get me wrong. I'm not suggesting going to extremes, such as becoming narcissistic. But the ego must be strong, not big, for you to do what you have to do, and that comes from self-confidence, self-esteem, and self-love. Then you can share that love. In fact, I believe it happens almost naturally.

Okay, let's talk about the *L* word. I know it's touchy-feely, but the most important things in your life are touchy-feely, aren't they? More on that later. What's most important to you? If you don't say family, you're probably reading this around your buddies. I'll wait for you to be alone, and then you'll say family. What keeps a family together? It's love, man! John and Paul were right: "All you need is love." Keep in mind there's a huge difference between love and lust. To put it in simple GI terms, love is unconditional giving. Lust is selfish wanting. Easy enough?

Every relationship can be measured by the amount of love shared. Think about it. (Yes, now I'm asking you to practice what I preach.) Your relationship with another person is strong because you're willing to give him or her all you can—all you have. You're willing to give without the condition that he or she give back to you. That's love! And there's incredible power in that! As I write this, my heart is saddened by the overwhelming number of our soldiers being killed in Iraq. Having been a warrior all of my adult life, I know that a soldier, airman, sailor, marine, or coast guardsman can do what is expected only through the strength gained from love of country, family, and fellow warriors. What can a person who puts his or her life on the line expect in return? Money? That's silly, isn't it? By now you should realize that you're in this not for the money or prestige, but because you love what you do and who you do it for. It's about relationships. It's about love!

Last of all, *the most important part of your life is spiritual.* Interestingly, when you've taken care of the physical, mental, and emotional areas, you'll find a sense of peace that empowers you to think beyond yourself. Maslow called it self-transcendence. It goes beyond self-actualization. I call it spiritual.

Often, people misconstrue spirituality with religion. It's not necessarily the same. If religion is the way by which you develop your spiritual life, then hallelujah! If it's not, don't worry about it. To me, spirituality is about opening your mind and your heart to appreciate all that abounds around you.

I currently live in Colorado, near Pikes Peak. Every morning I drive toward the west and get a glimpse of a giant postcard. I see what Katharine Lee Bates saw when she wrote the lyrics to "America the Beautiful"—from a different angle, of course. The mountains really are purple, and they are majestic! Paradoxically, one

41

of the most effective ways to get to the spiritual is to appreciate the natural. Go outside, whether in the sunshine or the snow, and listen and observe. Hear the birds or the wind. Feel the breeze. Nature will astound you with its beauty if you pay attention.

Another way to develop your spirituality is by thinking (there I go again, using the *T* word) about the value of the people with whom you live and work. Time has changed the risks of living in this world. There's a possibility—not a probability, I hope— that all of those people with whom you live and work and, possibly, those you love could get killed as you read this passage. God forbid, but the possibility does exist. We are not as safe as we used to be. Imagine—again, God forbid—that your friends or family were all killed. How would you feel? Would that not put you in a spiritual frame of mind?

Surely, we don't know what we'd do if a catastrophe like that befell us. In truth, we do know what we should do to express our appreciation and love for those with whom we share our lives. We often choose not to because we don't exercise our spirit. You can change that. Today. Right now.

I hope you'll practice this habit daily. It will affect you, and it will affect those with whom you live. If you choose to do nothing else I've commended to you, work on this habit. It will increase your life span, and it will give you peace. Take care of yourself so that you can take care of others who, in turn, will take care of you. Developing and maintaining these four basic areas of your life are critical to your ability to lead warriors. You have to have a sharp weapon. Denise Austin, the fitness guru, said it best: "Health is wealth!" Get rich! Take care of yourself first!

## War Story

I used to run a lot. (Okay, I jogged regularly. Man, I walked fast and often, okay? Well, maybe it wasn't as often as I used to think.) I was what someone once referred to as a seasonal runner. My running didn't have much to do with any season, though. I quit whether it was the right season or not. I'd run regularly for a couple of months, and then I'd go TDY for a few weeks, which gave me an excuse to quit for a couple of months—and then I'd do it all over again. It was tough starting over, but it was fairly easy quitting each time. In fact, like any habit, the more I quit, the easier it became. I was soon an exceptional quitter!

I've never been out of shape for long. Whenever I started feeling that way, I'd begin working out. This went on for many years. One day I was teaching Covey's *The 7 Habits of Highly Effective People* to a group of attorneys. As I talked about what I just shared with you, a young captain in the front row got excited and said, "You know, Chief, I have the same problem. If, however, you're willing to be my accountability partner, I'll make a commitment to start a physical fitness program if you will." I'm always up to a challenge. Hey, maybe I could outsmart a lawyer!

We agreed to work out for at least 20 minutes, three times a week, and connect with each other every Monday. We did just that. Every Monday morning, the captain would write, telling me how it had gone the previous week, and I'd lie and tell her I'd done my part. (Okay, I didn't always lie; I really did stick with it.) She had a harder time, due to her workload, I guess. I recall one note she sent after two weeks had elapsed. She'd not met her commitment. Hard charger that she was, however, she said she was on her way to the gym to work out for three hours to make up for it. I immediately called and convinced her she couldn't just make it up like that. The idea was to do it regularly. Amazingly, she agreed. She was eventually reassigned, so I lost touch with her. But I stuck with my program. I'd started riding a bike that goes nowhere—but fast. By the time we lost our connection, I had developed a habit of working out regularly on that bike. I do it to this day. (Or every other day.)

Do you know when men (generally speaking) start a no-kidding regular exercise program? After their first heart attack! If you've seen the movie *Something's Gotta Give*, you'll recall that Jack Nicholson's whole perspective on life changes when he has a heart attack. Why wait? Maybe we should attack the heart in a different way—by helping it instead of hurting it.

Let me tell you the truth. When I work out, when I ensure that I keep learning, when I'm grateful for myself and the people with whom I share my life, and when I appreciate Earth's unfathomable beauty, I'm invincible! I'm empowered with the strength, wisdom, courage, and grace to accomplish all that I set my heart and mind to. My sword is sharpened, and I know I'll win the battle! Hooah!

# Starting Points

- How can I improve or maintain my physical health?
- How can I improve or maintain my mental health?
- How can I improve or maintain my emotional health?
- How can I improve or maintain my spiritual health?

# Words of Wisdom

*Patience is also a form of action.*
—Auguste Rodin

*I have resolved that from this day on, I will do all the business I can honestly, have all the fun I can reasonably, do all the good I can willingly, and save my digestion by thinking pleasantly.*

—Robert Louis Stevenson

*The final forming of a person's character lies in their own hands.*

—Anne Frank

*Fifty years ago people finished a day's work and needed rest. Today they need exercise.*

—Unknown

*A man too busy to take care of his health is like a mechanic too busy to take care of his tools.*

—Spanish proverb

*The cyclone derives its powers from a calm center. So does a person.*

—Norman Vincent Peale

*Have you ever been too busy driving to stop to get gas?*
—Stephen Covey

*Rule your mind, or it will rule you.*
—Horace

# Habit 6

## Be Good!
### Know Your Stuff

Remember when Mom used to call out to you, "Be good!" as your little legs carried you out the door as fast as they could? Slamming the door behind you, you didn't pay much attention to her. Habit 6 resembles that scenario to some extent. It doesn't come from Mom (although I've been called a mother several times as I redirected folks). This habit has three basic parts. Let me begin by asking you a simple question: What do Michael Jordan, Mia Hamm, Tiger Woods, Brett Favre, Mary Lou Retton, Larry Bird, Magic Johnson, and Kareem Abdul-Jabbar all have in common? Yes, they are—or were—great athletes. What else? Look at the subtitle of this habit. They know their stuff! You may say that some of the "older" folks I listed *knew* their stuff, but that's only half true. The other half is that once you know your stuff, you'll always know it—you just use it in a different way. Older, indeed!

The athletes I listed are great because they are competent. That's the first part of being good. *To be good, you have to be competent!* Oh sure, professional athletes have God-given abilities we call talent, just as you do, but they have to hone that talent. You do that by using it and working on it. Great athletes work hard to develop and maintain their competence. Now that you've graduated to the real world and wear "butter" on your shoulders, do you think you won't have to work? Sorry to be the bearer of bad news. The truth is you'll have to work even harder to hone your technical skills because now they matter. In school what's the worst thing that could have happened if you had failed a test? As an officer/leader, the worst that can happen is that someone might die from your mistake. It might be you. So don't do that!

There is no substitute for competence. I'll share a war story with you that makes that point in a minute or two. A concept that has become very popular during the past few years is readiness—being prepared to go to war. How do you prepare? All of these habits you've been reading about enable your readiness. Specifically, when we talk about being good, readiness means being competent to do your job—to know your stuff.

I would be foolish to try to tell you how to hone your particular technical skills. You can do that by getting more training, reading, talking with experts, finding a mentor, or going back to school. (If you're an Air Force Academy grad, you don't even want to hear that one, do you?) Let me tell you that, as a new lieutenant, you will not have time to do these things—I guarantee you. You'll have to *make* time! The world and your work are changing at megaspeed. If you don't keep up, you'll be left behind. Do your part to maintain your competence, and develop a relationship with your troops that will empower them to keep you informed on new developments they learn about. Remember the web that Chief Seattle talked about? Help your troops help you. *Be competent!*

*The second part of being good has to do with character.* I can help you with that. (I've been called a character too!) I don't know what you do, but I do know who you are. You are a lieutenant. An officer. A warrior. A leader. Your ability to lead is as important as developing and maintaining your technical expertise. When you leave your unit, your troops won't remember what you did. They *will* remember who you were, based on how you treated them.

"Being" has to do with character. Chances are you've had some training in character development. If not in school, I'll assume you got some at home from the people who raised you. Since I don't know what you were taught, let me give you the truth. Basically, character means living up to your corps' values. Whether it's the Air Force's *Integrity, Service, and Excellence;* the Navy and Marines' *Honor, Courage, and Commitment;* or the Army's *Loyalty, Duty, Respect, Selfless Service, Honor, Integrity, and Personal Courage,* you must *embody* those values. They must come from your personal core—your heart—if you're going to be an Exceptionally Powerful Lieutenant.

Although you're expected to live up to all of the core values of your particular service, the most important is *integrity.* I believe that all the others grow from that one, just as your troops will grow from their experience with you. Integrity is often defined in terms of honesty. That's certainly part of it, but the critical element has to do with wholeness. When a vessel—whether a ship, tank, or plane—maintains its integrity, it's whole, and it can accomplish what it was made for. God knows, you don't want to be inside one of those vehicles when it loses its integrity! The vehicles you drive are important, but the vessels you lead are critical. Those vessels are you and your people.

What drives you? If it isn't the desire to do what's right, then reconsider your commitment to being an officer. Doing what's right is basically what integrity is about. To your enlisted troops, being good means doing what's right in all you do, all the time. Okay, I'm giving you the Air Force perspective, but I think it encapsulates all of the services' core values.

Doing what's right isn't always easy. Michael Josephson told me that character is "doing what's right even when it costs more than you're willing to pay." There's usually a price to pay for doing what's right, but it's worth it in the end. Remember when we talked about discipline as discipleship? Do you think you'll raise disciples if you don't do what's right?

Integrity is clearly a vital component of character development. We often define integrity as doing what's right *when no one is watching*. But what's right? It's not lying, not stealing, not cheating, and not letting anyone else do it either. Most of our military academies include those restrictions in their honor codes. Isn't character about honor?

Maintaining our honor isn't always easy. I think that the most difficult part is "not letting anyone else do it," don't you? That takes what I call moral courage. Turning in a buddy who has violated the code or done something illegal is probably the toughest test you'll have to pass. As a first sergeant, I had to reprimand my very best friend. I would have taken a bullet for him any day (and still would), but as the leader I had to do what was right— and it wasn't easy. Luckily he had plenty of integrity, which made it easier. "Bob," he said, "the troops are watching us. We need to do what we should. We can't breach our integrity, so let's get this done." He was much stronger than I. We're still brothers. *Having and exhibiting moral courage is key to being a good officer and critical to being a good leader.*

*The last part of being good is having confidence.* In truth, confidence will almost pour out of you if you're competent, if you're a person of good character, and if you exhibit moral courage. You may remember a commercial some years back—I believe it was an ad for a deodorant that warned you to "never let them see you sweat." In a way, that commercial made a great deal of sense. The product would help the user give an impression of confidence. Well, I don't know of any product that will give you confidence, but I do know that if you're competent and have good character, you'll be able to make tough decisions with the confidence that you've done what's right.

Know your stuff! Whether it's in what you do or who you are, make sure you know what you're doing to the best of your ability. You need to know your stuff, but not to impress your troops (they will know much more than you, even if they won't let on at first). You need to know your stuff as a leader and as an expert in your field because everything you do affects someone's life. If you don't know all you should, make sure to invest time in improving your skills. You are not at the top of the heap. On the contrary, you're at rock bottom again. Hey, don't worry. This won't be the first time. Life is a cycle. Once you make it to the top, you have to start at the bottom again. Be good at what you do and who you are.

## War Story

I'm old, so I had to go into the hospital for a "procedure." Have you ever noticed how medical folks use fancy terms for things like sucking the blood out of your veins or invading your body with an instrument much larger than the orifice they plan to stick it in? Okay, so I'm going in for this procedure that a "man my age" should have. Or so I'm told.

Now, I really needed this procedure, so it took only four months to get an appointment to talk to a doc about it. (Yeah, I go to a military hospital.) It would eventually turn into five months before I had fun. Therefore, the man my age was now a lot older. The doc was a good guy. He'd served 30 years before he started getting paid for what he did in the service for free. In other words, he was a retired GI like me. (Okay, enough editorializing.) I was very interested, to say the least, in what the procedure entailed. I'm sure my blood pressure increased as he explained what would happen. After he was done, he asked me if I had any questions.

"Doc, how many times have you done this?" "About 24,000," he answered, to my relief. "Has anyone ever died while you were doing it?" "No one," he said proudly, "yet." "Yet?" Doctors shouldn't try to be comedians. Imagine if he'd answered my question about how many times he'd done this procedure with "Oh, this my first time, but don't worry. I graduated at the top of my class, and I've read all the manuals!" No way! You ain't practicing on me, man! I suppose you have to start somewhere. Although I can't verify this, I've often heard that medics who work in immunizations practice on themselves. Some things you can't practice on yourself. You'll find that out in due time, when you're a person of my age and need this procedure.

The point of this story has to do with what I mentioned earlier. You have to know your stuff. Would you go to a doctor who hasn't been trained, one who doesn't know what he's doing? Of course not! Why not? Because he might kill you! It's the same in your business or businesses. You have to know your technical stuff so that you don't get someone killed, and you have to know your character stuff so you don't destroy someone's life, including your own. And you have to be confident that you've done what you should. If you noticed, as I described the doc who worked on me, I first mentioned that he was a good guy. I first tried to check out his character, but I also made sure he was technically competent. Based on how he answered my questions with great confidence, I felt that I could put my life in his hands. I survived the procedure, although he admonished me to see him again in five years. Well, if I ain't dead by then, maybe I'll go have more fun again. Be good! Lives depend on it!

## Starting Points

- Do I really know what I'm doing?
- Do I need more training?
- Do I embody my corps' values?
- Do I continuously do what's right?

# Words of Wisdom

*When you become a leader, you lose the right to think about yourself.*

—Gerald Brooks

*The final test of a leader is that he leaves behind him in other men the conviction and will to carry on.*

—Walter Lippmann

*Say what you mean, mean what you say, but don't say it mean.*

—Anonymous

*Never let a problem to be solved become more important than a person to be loved.*

—Barbara Johnson

*Nearly all men can stand adversity, but if you want to test a man's character, give him power.*

—Abraham Lincoln

*Doing the right thing for the right reason in the right way is the key to quality of life.*

—Stephen Covey

*Quality is never an accident; it is always the result of high intention, sincere effort, intelligent direction, and skillful execution; it represents the wise choice of many alternatives.*

—Willa A. Foster

*You cannot dream yourself into a character; you must hammer and forge yourself one.*

—James A. Froude

*Talent is a gift, but character is a choice.*

—John C. Maxwell

Habit 7

# **Build Trust!**
## **Be Trustworthy**

At the beginning of habit 6, I asked you to relive your days at home when Mom told you to be good. Now, I don't have the female perspective, never having been one, so forgive me if I sound sexist, but here's something all men go through. Recall, if you will, the first time Dad let you have the keys to the car so that you could go out on a date. Did he give you the "I brought you into this world, and I'll take you *out* and make a better one—and it'll be more fun this time!" talk? In case he didn't, let me play that role with you now.

Dad: "I'm trusting you with this vehicle that I've worked hard to pay for." (All dads are trained to say things in a way that will make their children feel guilty enough that they'll do the right thing.)

"I've sweated countless hours so that the family would have a decent car to travel in. Now, I'm going to trust you to take care of it. I know, however, that sometimes things happen." (Dads are also trained to practice tough love. The idea is to incorporate guilt with responsibility, hoping to produce integrity.)

"If something should happen to the car—for instance, if someone runs into you [notice he didn't say if you run into someone; that's different, and you will pay for it!]—I expect you to tell me about it." (Dad is saying, "Keep me informed." You'll see that again soon.)

"I'd rather you tell me about it than hear of it from someone else. Don't ever lie to me." (Now get ready for the coup de grâce.)

"I can deal with an accident happening; it happens to all of us." ("Yeah, right," you're thinking. "He's going to understand!" A good dad will.)

"What I won't put up with is your lying to me about it. Understand?" (Here's where he adds the "I brought you into this world, I'll take you out. . . ." for emphasis.)

Of course you understand, and you tell him so (although you hadn't yet read this book back then, so you didn't know how to listen—consequently, you shut him off eight seconds after he started).

That conversation has to do with building trust. *Trust is the most important thing you'll have to develop among your troops if you're going to be an Exceptionally Powerful Lieutenant.* Trust binds people together so they can accomplish whatever mission lies ahead.

Whom do we trust? Wait a minute. Before we get to that, let me ask you to define *trust*. Put the book down a minute, and think a little bit. Thanks for coming back. What comes to mind when I ask you to define that word? I'd bet my huge retirement paycheck that you said something to the effect that "trust is when people are honest" or "it's when people do what they say they will do." Am I close? I won't say that you're wrong, but let me get back to that issue after I answer the question "Whom do we trust?"

*We trust people who are competent, who are confident, who keep us informed, who listen to us, who are considerate (who care), who make themselves available, who are consistent, and who are principle-centered.* Let me tell you that trust is built from a combination of these eight traits. You can't build trust by doing only one of them. The more of them you have, the more trust you'll build. Let me address each one separately.

Habit 6 was about the importance of being technically and morally competent, which leads to confidence. I think you understand competence. Let me make just one more point on how confidence builds trust. Imagine if that doc I told you about in my war story came into the operating room scared and wondering if he could do what was expected of him that day. How long do you think I would have stayed on that operating table? I'd have been out of there in a New York minute! It's the same with leading your troops. Will they follow you if you're incompetent? Nope! Will they follow you if you're indecisive or show fear? Of course not! A scene in the movie *U-571*, which I'll refer to again in habit 8, illustrates what I'm talking about. You'll recognize it when you read about it in a few minutes. The scene depicts a conversation between a crusty Navy chief and the skipper. The point in that scene is that *we trust people who are competent, and we trust people who are confident.*

Recall that in my opening "Dad talk," I promised that you'd see "keep me informed" again. As a man of integrity, I have to live up to that promise, so here it is. The whole point of that conversation was that *we trust people who keep us informed regardless of the news, whether it's bad or good.* Truthfully, as a leader, you'll have more trust (if levels of trust exist) in those who give you bad news. Whom would you rather hear bad news from—one of your troops or the general? I rest my case. That's the point your dad was trying to make.

I already gave you my perspective on listening. Does it make sense that *we trust people who listen to us?* (Go ahead, "Nod your head like this," as rapper Will Smith would say.) I've also shared with you how *your troops will believe (trust?) in how you care.*

What about availability? Let me go back once more to your parents. I could be getting into a touchy area here. Forgive me if I do. I told you from the beginning that what I share with you is the truth as I know it. One of the greatest blessings I had growing up was that I had two parents. I still do, as I write, and I'm oh so grateful for that! Not only did I have both my parents but also they were always there when I needed them. I recall the enthusiasm with which Dad went to all of my concerts when I was in the band in junior high and high school. Have you ever heard a junior high or high school band? Okay, let me not offend anyone more than I have to. I'm being cynical when I refer to my dad's enthusiasm. But he was always there! He was always available, just as Mom was. I could always count on being able to talk to my parents about anything. Often they had no clue what I was talking about, but they would sit and listen. I hope you grew up in that type of environment. If you did, you know what I'm saying when I tell you *we trust people who are available.* Imagine having an open-door policy, but you're never there! Granted, if you're out finding your troops to take care of them, that's a good reason to be gone, but *you have to make yourself available to your troops if you're going to build trust.*

*If you make these eight lessons habits, they will lead you toward consistency.* When we talked about sharpening the sword, I mentioned the term *moody.* Have you ever lived or worked with a moody person? How was life? I'm putting these questions in the past tense, hoping that you're not living in that environment now. Moody people have a huge negative impact on the environment. You may be asking, "What about people who are consistently moody?" I guess you can at least trust that they won't be positive. I stay away from those folks! Be consistent in all of the positive things, and you'll build trust.

The final element for building trust—*being principle-centered*—goes back to your corps' core values. Principle-centered people live those core values daily. That's not always easy to do. Life is simple but not necessarily easy. Leadership is the same way. So many leaders preach their corps' values yet don't live up to them. Your troops will see right through that. Trust—the glue that keeps you together and moves you in the right direction—will fade quickly. Know the principles that your corps expects you to embody, and practice them daily in everything you do.

Let me share the truth with you again. The highest principle is love. I know that you don't want to get into that because you've been taught that warriors are macho, and this is a touchy-feely subject. Remember my asking you about what's most important to you? Your response was family. Isn't family touchy-feely? It is for most of us. Even your corps' values are touchy-feely because they have to do with touching others in a positive way, and it feels so good when everyone in the corps lives up to them. Let me remind you that I define the *L* word as *unconditional giving*. If you're principle-centered, you'll give all you have, unconditionally. You'll love your people and appreciate them for who they are, and they will do the same in return.

As I said before, it takes a combination of these behaviors to develop trust. The more of them you have, the more trust you will have—and the more effective you will be. Now let me give you the real lesson in trust. Remember when I asked you to define the term and you came up with ways others display trust? Here's the truth. The only way to develop trust is for *you* to be *trustworthy*. *You* have to do those eight things you nodded your head about. *You* have to be willing to make the effort to be trustworthy. Others don't develop trust. *You* do! Do it now!

## War Story

You're going to find this hard to believe, but I can be arrogant when I choose to. Yeah, yeah, I know you're thinking, "Say it ain't so, Chief!" I promised you the truth, and that's the truth, as much as it hurts you. Let me prove it to you.

The Fifteenth Air Force Band at March AFB, California, was my first assignment as a chief master sergeant. I was a bit proud of myself. I'd survived some events in my life that others had said would be fatal to my career. I'd beaten the odds and attained the highest rank in the Air Force's enlisted structure. I was in the top 1 percent of the enlisted force! To put it in the vernacular, I was a little "ate up" with myself.

In almost 20 years of service as a musician, I'd never had the opportunity to go home to play for my folks—all of those countless hundreds of people who lived in Deming, New Mexico, and whose last names ended in *uez*. That opportunity came shortly after I arrived at March. The band hadn't toured near my hometown, so my commander suggested that I take the big band there to show some homeboy-makes-good pride. Great idea!

Since that area of the Southwest was my turf, I decided to do the advance work, just to ensure a successful tour. I traveled to several small towns in southern New Mexico. (Okay, all towns in southern New Mexico are small.) Anyway, Deming was my last stop before returning to March. I did my work and stayed an extra day to be with my family. I hadn't seen some of my pals in years, so I went out searching for them. I was amazed at how many of my high school friends were still in town. (High school, by the way, was a great experience for me—the best six years of my life. Hey, I was an overachiever!)

As I told you at the beginning of this story, I can be arrogant. Look, my buddies made me that way. They'd gone nowhere in the past 20 years. Richey and Eddie Sainz, Hector Ochoa, Richard Acosta, and Charlie Sera had all stayed in our dinky little hometown doing what their dads had done all of their lives, which is what their dads' dads had done before. I, on the other hand, had already seen the world. I'd played for all of the presidents of the United States alive at the time! I'd been overseas! Man, I'd been to Burma! I was worldly! How could I not be arrogant? See? My friends made me that way! I enjoyed visiting with my old chums, but we just weren't the same anymore. I was in a different league now. I went back to California to coordinate the tour that would show my folks how well I'd done.

We started in northern Arizona and worked our way to central New Mexico. It was winter, and the weather didn't seem to want to cooperate with us. Not only did we have to load in and out in the cold and wet, but also we had long stretches of nothing but desert between towns. We played at Eastern New Mexico University near Silver City one night and left the next morning for New Mexico State University in Las Cruces, where we would perform that evening. What a blustery day! Twenty-five of us traveled in an MCI bus, following an 18-wheel trailer carrying tons of musical and electronic equipment. As we traveled down this two-lane winding highway through the middle of nowhere, we noticed that the equipment truck, a few miles ahead of us, had pulled over to the side. There wasn't much of a shoulder, but the driver had gotten out of the way as best he could. Wouldn't you know that all four cars registered in New Mexico happened to drive by that truck on that day! It was a tough situation, raining and cold. The truck—and now the bus—hindered traffic. You see, those four guys had never seen a situation like this, so they had to keep coming around to see what was happening.

The truck was "hard broke," a term airplane mechanics use that means "that vehicle ain't going *no*where!" All this happened in the days before anyone had ever asked, "Can you hear me now?" We had no cell phones and no way (other than driving 100 miles) to get to a phone to call for help. Luckily, a local sheriff (yes, he had a gun) stopped and carried me and an assistant to his office to call for a wrecker.

Unfortunately, it now seemed that there were more than four cars registered in New Mexico, and they were all broken down. Trucks with every local wrecker service I called were out and wouldn't be back for hours. I didn't have time to wait. The sheriff suggested calling one in Deming, the nearest town. (If you were paying attention, you'll remember that Deming is my hometown.)

I had no choice, so I called Sainz's Wrecker Service, the only one in town—Richard Sainz proprietor. Richey answered my call. (Again, if you were paying attention you'll recognize the name of one of my old buddies.) "Hey, Bobby!" he said after I announced myself, "How are you?" Well, we talked about other things than my predicament, but we did get to that topic eventually. I needed his help, and I needed it quickly. As we finished our conversation, Richey said, "I'll be right there!" And he was!

I don't know how he got there so quickly. Maybe it had something to do with all of the state cops being family, so he didn't have to worry about speeding.

On our way back to the truck and bus, I started thinking. Here I was, a top dog in my society—the Air Force. I commanded literally thousands of troops, had almost countless resources at hand, and had done things I can't tell you about without having to shoot you—all in all a highly successful life. Yet I was stuck with my team in the middle of the desert, and the only person available to help me was a skinny, unpretentious guy whom I had recently looked down on for not doing "more" with his life.

You'll recall all my allusions to humility. I was humbled to the bone. My friend Richey, a humble man himself, had come to my rescue and, in a sense, had rescued the entire United States Air Force by enabling us to accomplish our mission. That truck had major problems, but with the help of a few humble men, we finished the tour and returned to our home base safely.

Richey epitomized every aspect of building trust. He knew what he was doing, and he made sure I knew that he knew. He told me what he was going to do after grasping the severity of the problem. He never discussed payment; he just wanted to get us to where we needed to be. He was there when I needed him. He did his duty out of love and respect. He was, and still is, a warrior with whom I would go to war any day, anywhere. I trust him that much!

## Starting Points

- Am I trustworthy?
- Am I consistent?
- Do I share what I know with my troops and my bosses?
- Do I live my corps' values?

## Words of Wisdom

*Few things help an individual more than to place responsibility upon him and to let him know that you trust him.*

—Booker T. Washington

*Most of us know how to say nothing, but few of us know when.*

—Unknown

*Trust in what you love, and it will take you where you need to go.*

—Natalie Goldberg

*We're like blind men on a corner—we have to learn to trust people, or we'll never cross the street.*

—George Foreman

*We are at the center of a seamless web of mutual responsibility and collaboration.*

—Robert Haas

*You can't have science with one scientist.*

—Alan Kay

*The best proof of love is trust.*

—Joyce Brothers

*We have to build trust in peacetime so that we can assume it in wartime.*

—Maj Gen Gary "Dutch" Dylewski, USAF, Retired

# Habit 8

## **Hang on Tight!**
### **Find an Enlisted Mentor**

I'm sitting at my office desk when all of a sudden I hear a commotion in the offices across from mine. As I walk out to see what's the matter, I find a colonel yelling at the top of his voice at *my* lieutenant! This is unacceptable! I respectfully ask the colonel if he and I can speak in my office. He, of course, agrees. (You don't say no to a chief.) In my office, I ask the colonel not to do what he just did. As diplomatically as I can, I tell him, "Sir, whatever my lieutenant did, I'm sure he didn't do it intentionally. He's a good man, so you can converse with him in a civil manner, and he will give you all he has. Please show him the respect he's due." "You're right, Chief. I was upset and wasn't thinking. Thanks!" The colonel then went out and talked with—not to—my lieutenant, who took care of him. As the colonel left the building, my lieutenant came into my office and thanked me for saving his butt. He didn't need to thank me. He was *my* lieutenant!

Remember the scenes in the movie *We Were Soldiers* in which the young soldier walks by SGM Basil Plumley, played by Sam Elliott? The young man says, "Good morning, Sergeant Major!" Plumley responds, "How the *#^& would you know what kind of morning this is?" Later, the same thing happens, and Plumley again says something unprintable. I think the movie director was trying to make a point. The sergeant major is depicted as tough—maybe even crude. I'm not sure sergeants major or other senior noncommissioned officers (SNCO) are quite that way anymore. Oh, they're just as tough all right, but maybe not as crusty.

In developing your leadership skills, consider this: Whom will you lead? Enlisted folks! Who in the military world could better tell you about the people you'll lead than an enlisted person? This is not rocket science. Yes, that's right! An enlisted person will give you the best guidance. Now wouldn't it be smart—and we've already concluded that you *are* smart—to find one who's "been there"? That would probably be an SNCO. Let me say, though, that plenty of middle-tier and junior NCOs can mentor you, but they may not be as seasoned as an SNCO. The point is that if you're going to be an Exceptionally Powerful Lieutenant, find an enlisted mentor and hang on tight!

Here are a couple of other examples that Hollywood has blessed us with. How about the scene in the movie *Glory*, right after Col Robert Gould Shaw (Matthew Broderick) has flogged Private Trip (Denzel Washington) for "deserting"? Whom does Shaw go to for advice? He seeks out Gravedigger (Morgan Freeman), who is obviously the most mature of his enlisted men. Colonel Shaw sees his value and seeks his counsel. In fact, Gravedigger is so good that Shaw makes him a sergeant major! Who knows enlisted folks? Enlisted folks! Find one fast!

Let's go back to *We Were Soldiers*. Recall, if you will, the part in which Lt Col Hal Moore, played by Mel Gibson, is at his wit's end. He can't get out of his situation, and it seems that he and his troops are destined to reenact the fate of the famous (infamous?) 7th Cavalry (George Custer's former unit). He looks at Sergeant Major Plumley, who's been with him the entire battle, and asks, "I wonder how Custer felt?" Plumley looks straight at him and says, "Sir, Custer was a weenie (he uses a different word). You ain't!" This immediately reenergizes Colonel Moore to reach inside and do what he has to do to save his troops.

Maybe the best example of this idea of holding on tight to a seasoned SNCO is the scene in *U-571* in which young lieutenant Andrew Tyler (Matthew McConaughey) becomes the submarine's skipper by default after the commander is killed. The lieutenant isn't doing very well at leading his men. Over a cup of coffee, CPO Henry Klough (Harvey Keitel) asks the lieutenant for permission to speak freely. The skipper, of course, does so. The chief admonishes him, saying, "The commanding officer is a mighty and terrible thing, a man to be feared and respected. All knowing. All-powerful. The skipper always knows what to do whether he does or not." Will you always know what to do? Probably not, but you'll have a better idea if you're close to someone who has much more experience than you do—who knows your followers and has led them before. Don't you think? Find that someone fast, and hang on tight!

*You'll need a Sergeant Major Plumley, a Gravedigger, or a chief in your military life if you're going to be a successful leader.* You've probably been told by more experienced officers to find a trust-worthy SNCO and learn as much as you can from him or her. If you follow no other advice, do follow that counsel!

Do you remember that in habit 1 I mentioned the two types of enlisted folks you'll find in your unit (those who need you to lead them and those whom you need to follow)? When you come into my unit, I don't care whether you were the top graduate. I don't care if you won athletic awards at the academy. I don't even care where you got your commission. What I care about is whether you can lead or follow. I know you can't lead because you haven't had the experience to do so yet. So you'd better be able to follow. Now, here's the trick. If you're willing to follow me, I'll make you a great leader. I'll take you under my wing and help you excel. Recall my story at the beginning of this les-son. To get to *you*, they'll have to get through *me*. Senior en-listed professionals are a bit parochial in that they'll fight for what's theirs. If you're *my* lieutenant, I'm not going to let any-one or anything harm you! I'm responsible for your success. Now, combine your education with my experience. Is that a formula for exceptional leadership? I think you'll agree. Here's what will happen: all the time that you're following me, I'm making sure that everyone in the unit—and anywhere else—knows you're the leader. It's another circle. You see, I don't need to tell everyone that I'm a leader; they already know that. I'll make sure they know that you're the boss. And I'll make sure they know that if they mess with you, they mess with *me*! As I've said before, there are two people you don't want to mess with. Okay, there are now *three*!

I hope that by reading this book, you've come to the conclu-sion that humility is a common thread which connects all of these habits. Exceptionally powerful leadership requires a whole bunch of humility; therefore, Exceptionally Powerful Lieuten-ants are humble.

The central core value that the US Air Force tries to live up to is service before self. Humility grows from a person who strives to serve others before serving himself or herself. It also comes from realizing how little one knows, especially compared to the combination of experience, knowledge, and wisdom of others. Lastly, it grows out of understanding and valuing others. The point here is that you should humble yourself to an enlisted person who can show you the ropes and guide you to success. That doesn't mean you relinquish your responsibilities or authority. It means, in fact, that you strengthen them by sharing them.

Now, let me be very honest for a moment and tell you that not all enlisted folks will be good mentors. But you're no dummy. You now know how to listen, and you know what it takes to be an effective leader, assuming you put those other seven habits into action. So you can find an enlisted mentor whose purpose is the same as yours—to serve. Together, you will do great things!

One of the most poignant ceremonies we perform in the Air Force occurs hundreds, often thousands, of times a day. The other services probably have a similar ceremony. It's quite simple, but it illustrates the critical connection between officers and enlisted folks. Let me paint the picture for you. As you know, the mission of the Air Force has to do with flying airplanes. Flying starts with taking off. The pilot, an officer, will jump into the cockpit (the old guys will crawl into it), put the key in the ignition, and crank up the plane. (Okay, it's not quite that way, but you might understand what I'm saying better if I use that example.) Anyway, the pilot's in the seat, ready to go. Just before he or she takes off the emergency brake to start down the runway, an Airman (formerly an NCO) stands tall near the nose of the aircraft and gives the pilot a thumbs-up, signifying that the airplane is in tip-top shape and will get that pilot, crew, and anything else in that plane to their destination safely. The Airman then comes to attention and salutes sharply, solidifying the bond between the officer and the enlisted person.

Here's the lesson. Find an enlisted mentor whom you can trust to tell you the truth, even if it hurts. Learn as much as you can from that person, and share your knowledge with others. Remember that trust is a two-way street that starts with you. Take care of that troop, and he or she will take care of you. Know this: enlisted folks *always* take care of their officers. If you treat them with respect, they'll return it in spades. If you mess with them, they'll take care of you. Enough said.

# War Story

I was working at my desk at Ramstein AB, Germany, just before the Air Force threw me out. (I did *not* retire; that would require a voluntary action.) My teenaged daughter, Elyse, was sitting in a chair next to the door. As the support-group superintendent, I worked closely with several officers, one of whom turned out to be my favorite lieutenant in the whole world. (I'll just call him lieutenant so that I don't embarrass Lt Eric Carrano.) As I worked, the lieutenant came into my office several times asking for information, direction, money, and so forth. Every time he walked in, I stood up. My daughter watched this interaction for a while before asking me,

"Dad, why do you stand up every time the lieutenant comes in here?"

"He's an officer, Baby, and I'm an enlisted person. That's what enlisted people do." (I could tell that she was a little confused.)

"Aren't you a big guy in the Air Force, Dad?"

"Yeah," I said, wondering where she was going with this conversation.

"And isn't he a little guy?"

"Yeah, in a way."

"So why do you stand up for him? Shouldn't he stand up for you?"

Here's what I told her. (Hey, she asked for it, so I *had* to give her the sermon!) An enlisted person is supposed to stand up for an officer when the officer enters the enlisted person's presence. That's what the book says. Well, I was an active duty chief for about a dozen years, and the book never stopped me from going beyond it, if you know what I mean. I made it a habit to stand for *everyone* who came into my office. I still do so even though it's become more difficult as the knees age. It was—and still is—a sign of respect, regardless of rank. The way I see it, we all may have different functions, but each of us has the same value. Some would say that enlisted folks stand for officers as a sign of subordination. That's crap! No one is subordinate to anyone else. God made us all equal. In fact, one of the charters of a professional warrior is to support and defend the constitution of the United States, which states that we are created equal. Subordination creates negative energy. Humility creates positive energy. Subordination is maintained by an external source. It's involuntary. Humility comes from inside of us. It's real power because we choose it! I've never subordinated myself to anyone, and I never will.

I didn't stand *for* the lieutenant; I stood *with* him! Interestingly, he stood up when I went to him too. We didn't stand *for* each other; we stood *with* each other. The combination of my power and his created a third, much greater, power that would break apart without one of us. I knew that my "place" was to stand *for* him, but my strength was to stand *with* him. I hope that this explanation gives you a sense of my point. A powerful leader is humble. He or she realizes that power lies in helping and supporting others. The more you expand your support, the stronger your leadership power will be because the more people you give to, the more people will give to you. Humility is key to powerful leadership. End of sermon!

I hope I made my point with my daughter and with you. We all have to work together to accomplish anything worthwhile. Don't make the mistakes others have—learn from them. The more seasoned an enlisted person is, the more mistakes he or she has made that you can learn from. The enlisted force *is* the backbone of every service. I say that with all humility. That backbone will support you and make you the head if you do what you should. You'll surely find that the bond you develop with that enlisted mentor will last forever. Years later, several promotions later, you'll need that expertise, and you'll make a call or send an e-mail. You'll find that the relationship hasn't changed from the time when you served together. It's almost amazing. We are all connected. Strengthen those connections. Hang on tight!

## Starting Points

- Is my ego strong enough to follow an enlisted mentor?

- Am I willing to trust my enlisted mentor to tell me the truth, even if it hurts?

- Can I be honest with my enlisted mentor?

- Do I expect my enlisted people to stand *for* me or *with* me?

# Words of Wisdom

*If I have been able to see farther than others, it was because I stood on the shoulders of giants.*

—Sir Isaac Newton

*The block of granite, which was an obstacle in the path of the weak, becomes a stepping-stone in the path of the strong.*

—Thomas Carlyle

*It is necessary for us to learn from others' mistakes. You will not live long enough to make them all yourself.*

—Adm Hyman G. Rickover

*Change is inevitable; growth is intentional.*

—Glenda Cloud

*A great teacher never strives to explain his vision. He simply invites you to stand beside him and see for yourself.*

—Rev. R. Inman

*He who is afraid to ask is ashamed of learning.*

—Danish proverb

*We must all hang together, or assuredly we shall all hang separately.*

—Benjamin Franklin

# Final Thoughts

In this book, I have tried to give you a view from the eyes and hearts of the enlisted folks you'll soon be leading. Enlisted people think differently than officers—and rightly so. I may have said it before, but here it is again: enlisted personnel and officers have different functions but the same value. You will die without your enlisted folks, or you will have great military careers with them. It's your choice. Make the right one. As you do that, think about the eight habits I've commended to you. Develop and employ them so that the troops you lead will think and say, "I'll go to war with my Exceptionally Powerful Lieutenant any day, anywhere."

As I said in the preface, these thoughts are based on more than 30 years' experience in dealing with lieutenants of every sort. My hope is that you'll take these lessons and really turn them into habits. The more you do, the more powerful you will become. In addition to these eight habits, you'll need four assets to become truly powerful. I didn't include them as habits because they're a little different. You can develop habits. I'm not sure you can develop what I'm about to share with you. I think that you discover them. I can't give them to you; they'll come from deep inside you. They are *desire, capacity, will,* and *action.*

In habit 1, I told you that you can live that first-day scenario, but you have to make it so. In habit 8, I mentioned that humility is powerful because it's a choice. If you're going to be an Exceptionally Powerful Lieutenant, you must begin your quest with the *desire* to be one. That desire will grow out of your purpose. Remember that I asked you whom you will lead as a lieutenant? I asked you several times because it's a critical question. The answer is still enlisted folks. If your purpose is to take care of your charges, your enlisted people, the desire to be your very best will surface. You can be an Exceptionally Powerful Lieutenant if you desire it. You'll need three other assets though.

Wherever you go, the environment will be different than the one you just left. Thank goodness, huh? What you do and how you do it may be totally different. The one thing that won't change is you! Let me repeat myself. I don't know what you're going to

67

do, but I know who you're going to be. A lieutenant! An Exceptionally Powerful Lieutenant, I hope! You have the *capacity* to do whatever you desire. Habits 4, 5, and 6 will help you hone that capacity. You may encounter obstacles that could hinder you, including people who will work at keeping you from fulfilling your dreams. Don't let them stop you. Find that NCO or another mentor, regain your strength, and express your power. It's within you! You can be an Exceptionally Powerful Lieutenant if you desire. You have the capacity!

You may have the desire and the capacity to excel, but you're going to have to find the *will* to do so. You'll have to find it in your heart. Some of the habits, particularly 2 and 3, may take a great deal of willpower to attain. If you've already developed bad habits, you'll have to work twice as hard to replace them with good ones. But you can do it! At times your progress will stall. Don't give up. You can be an Exceptionally Powerful Lieutenant if you desire. You have the capacity! Find the will!

Finally, none of this will have any effect whatsoever unless you *do something*! Indian yogi and guru Paramahansa Yogananda said that "a wish is desire without energy." You can sit back on your butt, wishing all day long—but nothing will change. Or you can get off your "buts" and make great things happen. "But I can't!" "But I don't know how!" "But what if I fail?" If you fail, learn from it. As John C. Maxwell says, "Fail forward!" Progress requires *action*. You can be an Exceptionally Powerful Lieutenant if you *desire*. You have the *capacity*! Find the *will*! *Do it now*!

I wish you an exceptionally successful life as a lieutenant and beyond. I hope that you will pass on what you learn to others so that our forces will continue to grow. The profession you've volunteered to pursue is the most honorable of all professions. You'll never be fully compensated for the sacrifices you and your family will make in your pursuit to serve, but in the end your legacy will be one that very few people even dream of. Let me leave you with a thought from American author and clergyman Edward Everett Hale; it encapsulates all I said in the previous pages:

> I am only one, but I am one. I cannot do everything, but I can do something. And because I cannot do everything, I will not refuse to do the something that I can do. What I can do, I should do. And what I should do, by the Grace of God, I will do.

If you have comments or questions about what you have read, feel free to contact me at bobvasquez@heirpower.com.

May you become an Exceptionally Powerful Lieutenant! May God bless you! And may God bless America! ¡Adelante!

# Heirpower!

## Eight Basic Habits of
## Exceptionally Powerful Lieutenants

*Air University Press Team*

*Chief Editor*
Marvin Bassett

*Copy Editor*
Sherry C. Terrell

*Book Design and Cover Art*
Daniel M. Armstrong

*Composition and
Prepress Production*
Vivian D. O'Neal

*Quality Review*
Mary J. Moore

*Print Preparation*
Joan Hickey

*Distribution*
Diane Clark

Made in the USA
San Bernardino, CA
22 October 2015